# HOW TO SELL
# NOTHING

## THE LOGICAL WAY TO MAKE
## THE EMOTIONAL SALE

# JOE PALLO

INDIE BOOKS
INTERNATIONAL®

The E.A.R.N.I.N.G. The Sale System™ is a pending trademark of Joe Pallo.

ISBN 13: 978-1-952233-82-1
Library of Congress Control Number: 2021923341

Designed by Steve Plummer

INDIE BOOKS INTERNATIONAL®, INC.
2511 WOODLANDS WAY
OCEANSIDE, CA 92054
www.indiebooksintl.com

# CONTENTS

# Foreword

I N YOUR HANDS, you hold a blueprint for your future self. Whatever you need, want, and dream about is within your grasp—if you adopt a new way of thinking, listening, making decisions, and acting. Joe shares a unique philosophy with proven-to-work practices, strategies, ideas, and tactics. It is nothing short of astounding and can immediately impact your work, career, and life. In fact, what you want tomorrow, can start today when you apply the suggestions revealed in this book.

Joe is a rare individual, and it is an honor to see where he is today. When he was with the Tom James Company, I was his client, and he sold me a suit. It is a privilege to get a first read of his book. My hope is you will read carefully, take good notes, make smart decisions, and move on to the business of earning. Repeat. Repeat. Succeed!

It is not for the faint of heart. The stories and strategies revealed in this book will hold up a mirror to what you will do or will not do. We all sell something, or according to the book of Joe, we all sell nothing. How well you sell nothing will ultimately determine how successful you will become. Unfortunately, many will read a chapter or two and set it aside for a rainy day. I hope you will devour this book and refer to it often. The genius is in its simplicity and street-smart approach to making something great happen. It will help you lay a foundation for your potential to emerge, and you will flourish in every part of your work and life.

If you ever get a chance to meet Joe and hear him speak, you will never be the same. Audiences across North America have felt his presence and become more impactful because of his expertise. If you are a meeting planner or executive looking for a message that will impact your people or your team, book Joe to speak. You will be glad you did, and your people will thank you.

They will discover what it means to set themselves apart from their competition and how easy it can be to start, strengthen, and cement critical relationships with prospects, clients, and referral partners.

MARK LeBLANC, CSP
AUTHOR OF *NEVER BE THE SAME* AND *GROWING YOUR BUSINESS!*
EDINA, MINNESOTA

# Preface

It was the summer of 1997. I was a broke student who needed to make enough money to pay for my next year of college at North Dakota State. I knew nothing about sales, yet I decided to spend my summer with Southwestern Advantage selling books door-to-door. It was a straight commission gig. I worked in Charlotte, North Carolina, and I didn't even have a car. I decided that I would be dumb enough to be smart enough to do exactly what they said; I thought that if I failed, it would be their fault. It was not an easy job, selling door-to-door, eighty hours a week in North Carolina in the summer. Never is, but there was a bright spot. On Sundays, we had a fun day or a day off where we did something, like go to an amusement park.

It was my first week out and it didn't go tremendously well. My sales manager Jay Stibbe gave me a copy of Dale Carnegie's *How to Win Friends and Influence People*[1] and said, "Read this," which I did. I was at an amusement park, with tons of kids around having fun, and I parked my butt on a bench and started reading it. I imagined people walked by thinking, "That poor kid, he has no friends, how sad." Others probably thought, "What a loser." I didn't care; I had no choice. I had to figure this sales thing out or I would starve.

I dove into the book, and it was an awesome, easy read, and it changed my thinking. That one book had a huge influence on me. It guided me to where I was in the top 5 percent in the nation, a top rookie, and it hasn't stopped. I have read and reread it countless times since. What a cool thing for Dale Carnegie to have that much of an impact on people.

I am not fooling myself that *How To Sell Nothing* is anywhere near that level, but I do like the idea of influencing people. If you are looking for a literary piece of art, please put this book down and grab another. Think of this book as a mechanics repair guide where you can read it cover to cover or jump to the piece that needs fixing. It is meant to be used, have grease stains on it, and the corners dog-eared—something that you can refer to as needed.

We have all heard that sales or selling is the transference of feelings, or that the sale is based on emotions or the relationship. These feelings, emotions, and relationships can't be seen or touched. They are in a very real sense—nothing. Nothing at all. Thus, this book presents a logical way to successfully sell nothing.

Let's start with some ground rules. You know more about selling your product or services than almost everyone else does. You are the expert.

The ideas you will read in this book are designed to do two very specific things for you:

1. Help you sell more.

2. Help you sell better by establishing a relationship and engaging emotionally.

That means when you are telling your story, you make sure to tell it to open-minded people who want to listen and be emotionally engaged. That means the relationship has started, and they are beginning to fill their emotional bucket.

The result is increased sales, growth, and income, along with more fun, satisfaction, and a sense of accomplishment. Keep that in mind as we progress.

With that said, here are the three core beliefs behind *How To Sell Nothing*:

> *Core 1:* It is much easier to sell what they want to buy than selling what you want to sell.

> *Core 2:* The act of buying is based on two sales: The logical and the emotional. Both are needed, but the more important one is emotional as it makes the sale happen. The logical confirms or affirms the sale. A sale will only be made when they are emotionally engaged. Most people sell by using logic, yet when you sell with emotion, the emotions make the sale happen.

> *Core 3:* Selling is like using a recipe. You will get your desired result if you follow the directions and use the proper ingredients. If you mix up the order, such as baking everything first, then you will have a large pile of unmixed goo. Follow the proper sales process and odds are you will make the sale. With that said, if two cakes from the same recipe taste slightly different, it's because one cook added extra seasoning. It is the same in sales. This difference is the personal touch—each salesperson makes the sale slightly different. It is this mix of emotion and relationship that really makes the sale.

As you read this book, you will probably say, "Wait, I have heard this before," or "I know this." That is true. The person who invented sales died a long time ago, and since then, not much has changed.

You would no doubt agree that most of the good ideas in sales are known to everyone. The question you must ask yourself is this:

*Am I doing them on a regular basis?*

Even though you may have heard these ideas and principles many times before, odds are you are not consistently doing them daily. Or worse, you may not truly know you are doing them.

Remember, the goal here is to simply help you sell better and sell more. That means you let people buy. There is no arguing that that is the top priority.

Salespeople always want to know the key to success in sales, but there isn't just one key or one technique or one approach that always works.

Everything you will read here is about increasing your success by 1 to 2 percent. That may not seem like a lot, but if you add up many of these little 1 to 2 percent changes, it isn't very long until you have something pretty big.

In sales, as in life, we want things to be perfect. We plan, we rehearse, and we act—but life doesn't always work as it should, right?

Success in selling is not perfect or planned. It's actually pretty messy, hard, and sometimes unexpected.

Do not look for perfection because perfection does not exist. Instead, look for progress. Be better today than you were yesterday. Keep adding those 1 to 2 percent improvements together, day after day, and you will find the success you seek.

Years ago, when I worked at the Tom James Company, we had a sales training seminar. The speaker was Matt Parsons, my manager, and he asked a coworker of mine to put a piece of masking tape on a wall as high up as he could jump. My friend took the piece of tape, jumped, and stuck it on the wall. It was probably eight feet off the ground.

Matt asked, "Are you sure that was as high as you could jump?"

Taking another piece of tape, he tried it again, and he made it higher.

Then Matt challenged him a third time to focus really hard and do his absolute best to put the third piece of tape as high as possible.

My friend backed up and took a running start. He cleared the first two pieces of tape by several inches.

The obvious lesson is that it usually takes someone else's encouragement to get more out of us. With my sales coaching, as with any mentoring relationship, that is the case as well. Growth, over and beyond what is expected, is what we are going after. It's what we want as a result of a coaching relationship. That is the goal of this book.

But there is also a secondary lesson of removing limits and changing the way you may think. You have goals, dreams, and desires that are far bigger than the next sale. You can jump high on the wall with your piece of tape, but when you think differently, you act differently. Often we need someone else's help. For example, what would happen if you stood on someone's shoulders, used a ladder, or stuck the tape on a pole? There are no limits when you change your thinking. *How to Sell Nothing* was written to change your thinking.

Everyone has their own source of motivation. The point is there is always more behind the scenes. It is your motivating *why* that drives you, always moving you forward. The more you are in tune with what drives you, the more easily you will hit any sales goals. What you want is important, but why you want it is *extremely* important.

JOE PALLO
JUNE 2023

# PART I

# WHY SELLING NOTHING MATTERS

# 1

# What's Behind The Curtain?

**W**HEN I WAS young, skinny, and foolish (now I'm just foolish), I sold custom clothing to C-level executives for several years as a sales rep with the Tom James Company. It was a good gig. I did well, and I loved my time there. My business was 100 percent referral-based, meaning I was selling while seeing friends all the time.

One day I sold several custom suits and shirts to a gentleman named Dick Cochrane. Naturally, I asked for referrals and received four of them. When I returned to my office, I called the first name on the list, Mike Reier. I was lucky with the call, and the secretary put me through to Mike. I started my pitch by mentioning the person who gave me his name, and as I was getting into it, Mike suddenly cut me off and said, "Not interested," and he hung up the phone.

Yes, it did happen; someone did hang up on me. It does happen to all of us.

I figured Mike was having a bad day, so I moved on and called the next name on the list, Marty Fitterman. I got lucky again, and Marty answered. I told him I would be in his building the next day (he didn't know it, but I was going to be there to see him) and booked a meeting.

Our meeting went great, and Marty became a client. He also gave me four referrals, and one of those names was none other than Mike Reier.

When I returned to my office, I settled down to call all the referrals. I figured Mike must have been having a bad day yesterday, and he could not possibly be having a bad day two days in a row, so I called him again. I kind of "sold" myself on the idea that today would be the best day to call Mike.

I called him and was connected to him again. After I reminded him that we had talked yesterday, I said in addition to Dick Cochrane mentioning his name, Marty Fitterman had done so as well that very day. Mike replied, "I told you I am not interested." Another phone hung up on me.

Now, my dad says I am stubborn. My brother has said I am stubborn. And all of my sisters have said I am stubborn. In fact, my wife says I am stubborn. Even my kids say I am stubborn. But they are all wrong. And I will prove them wrong, even if it kills me.

With Mike, my stubbornness took root and flourished. I decided then and there that I would sell him no matter what. It became my mission. Every time I sold someone in that office who was connected in any way to him, I asked if they knew Mike Reier. I sold most, if not all, of his coworkers, a lot of his friends, and even sold to several of his neighbors.

Every time I was referred to Mike, I would call him and leave a message, telling him exactly who had mentioned his name and saying we should meet. I even had several of my clients' wives call Mike's wife and brag to her about me.

This went on for eighteen months. It got to be like a game. It was done professionally and with humor.

One day I came into my office, and the light on the phone was blinking. It was Mike Reier. He said, "Joe, you obviously are not going away, so please call my assistant and ask her to set something up."

I called her immediately. I set up the meeting, and just before I hung up, I asked if Mike was in.

When she said, "Yes, he is in," I heard Mike in the background say, "What does he want now? Yeah, put him through."

He kind of blasted me with his, "What do you want?"

"Mike, are you a busy guy?"

"Yes," he stated.

"Well, I want to take a few minutes to ask you a few questions to save us some time when we meet."

"Go ahead," he replied.

I then proceeded to qualify Mike and did my data gather for information so I would be prepared when we met.

A few days later, it was time to see Mike. I put on my favorite suit, organized my fabrics, and ensured I was prepared. I even pulled over a block away, dusted off my sales talk, and reread it.

In my mind, Mike was already sold. I was not leaving without him buying something from me. I was 100 percent convinced he would buy.

I am fairly sure Mike was 100 percent convinced he would not buy. I imagine he thought, "If I let Joe in and let him give me his pitch, I can say 'no,' and he will leave me alone."

That poor guy—he didn't stand a chance.

When we were establishing rapport, I was on point, dropping names—after all, I had sold almost everyone he knew. I answered objections in advance, getting him to tell me what he did, how much he traveled, what he didn't like about shopping, what he liked about his suits, and more.

After about fifteen minutes, we had several suits laid out, a dozen custom shirts picked, and several ties on the desk. He stopped and looked at me and said, "Joe, you are one of these," as he held out his hand in front of me.

"Mike, I am not sure what that means."

"You are one of the five best salespeople I have ever met," he explained, referencing the five fingers on his hand.

It was a nice compliment, a genuinely nice compliment, but it did not get in the way of my selling. "Thanks," I said, "and I am going to need the names and numbers of the other four people, and we need to look at a few sport coats while we are here."

I walked out of there with a good-sized order and four referrals. It took some time to finally get to Mike, but I accomplished my goal.

## DIG DEEPER TO GO HIGHER

Despite making the sale, something didn't feel right. My mind went to work to try and sort out my feelings. This sale was something I worked on for eighteen months. It was a great transaction. I got four referrals, and I received a tremendous compliment.

I stopped. It was the compliment that bothered me. Yes, it was a genuine compliment, but something about it rubbed me the wrong way.

After a few days of thinking about it and asking myself questions, I figured it out.

It bothered me that I could be thought of as only a great salesperson, or worse, that I could be known *only* as a great salesperson. I wanted to be known for more than that.

Naturally, I asked myself, "So, what do I want to be known for?"

I pondered that for a while and eventually asked myself another question, "Who are the top people I admire? Who has influenced me the most?"

After all, I reasoned that if I wanted to be known for something, that "something" would surely show up in the people I admired.

I began to wonder who influenced me the most and who had the biggest impact on me that I've met.

I started listing all the people who had helped or influenced me and then narrowed it down to the top five. The top five most influential people in my life are the following:

## 1—John Vito Pallo

He is my dad. When I was nine years old, my mother passed away. My life, along with those of my sisters and brother, was changed forever. Dad showed us the importance of never giving up and that everything happens for a reason. You must have faith. He is a great example of how to work hard and what it means to have character. He is one of my best friends.

## 2—Father Robert Schneider

He was the principal at Loyola High School in Mankato, Minnesota. I found myself in his office numerous times during my four years there. Most of the topics discussed were unpleasant for me, but he unintentionally taught me about leadership and how important it is to act.

We had a senior lounge—an empty classroom where seniors could gather before and after school or during our free periods. One morning as we came in, we found it was locked. I went to Dave Mettler, the custodian, to have him unlock it. Dave explained that Fr. Schneider told him to lock it. I went down to the principal's office with a buddy, Paul Schueneman, and asked if we could have the lounge unlocked. He said someone had left the chairs piled in the middle of the room, which was a fire hazard. (These chairs were old, like Catholic-school old. I even think Noah had them on the ark.) "If we promise not to do that again, can we have it unlocked?" I asked. He agreed. Later in the day, after senior mass, he mentioned, "Your class leaders promised me you would take care of the senior lounge and treat it properly."

I suddenly realized he was talking about me. He didn't mention any names, but I knew he was talking about me and Paul. He thought I was a leader, and he even said so. Leaders act. Leaders do. And you can't be a leader if you don't act, for true leadership is action. In addition, I learned you can be a leader and not even be aware of it. To this day, I am not sure my fifty-seven classmates ever thought of me as a leader, but it didn't matter because I acted. I bet some of them will read this and say, "Who is this guy?"

## 3—Spencer Hays

He was the majority shareholder of both Tom James and Southwestern Advantage (a door-to-door book sales company). My professional and personal worlds are based on the principles I learned while I worked at those companies. Much of what I hold dear is a derivative of applying those principles. Even how I interact with other people is based on what his companies taught me. Anyone who knows Spencer knows this story:

Every morning, he would wake up and say, "I feel healthy, I feel happy, I feel terrific." He then looked in the mirror and said, "You good-looking thing, you, don't you ever die." He was a great example of how to live life, how to control your attitude, and how to think big. He died in 2017 at age eighty.

## 4—Steve Gray

He was my sales manager at Tom James and taught me the importance of raising confident kids. I remember we were on an awards trip, whitewater rafting in Colorado, and Steve and I were having refreshments afterward.

He told me about his two kids, Cody and Kelsey, and how he tried to instill confidence in them.

At that time, I didn't have kids (I think I was just engaged), but what he said resonated with me. Years later, when I brought my firstborn home, I started a tradition of giving a kiss and saying, "Daddy loves you" and "You're neat." As my kids got older, I added things like, "You're important," "You're fun," "You are clever," and "I like spending time with you." I did this with each of my kids. I now have confident kids; at times, they may be too confident, but that is a good problem.

Steve is also one of the most straightforward, honest, dependable people I have ever known. He can always be counted on and will always do the right thing, even when it's inconvenient. Remember the "What would Jesus do?" bumper sticker? If I am ever in a quandary about what I should do, I ask myself, "What would Steve Gray do?" and know the right answer. He didn't realize the impact of his words until I told him about it many years later.

## 5—Lisa Pallo

She is my wife. I'm not 100 percent sure if I want her to know just how much she has made me a better man, father, and husband—and she is not done with me yet. She shows me every day what a tremendous mom and wife is like. She demonstrates daily that she is fantastic. She is my best friend, she puts up with me, and she is truly a wonderful person. I am lucky to have her. I am sure when Lisa reads this she will think, "I influence Joe? I can't even get him to put his dirty socks in the hamper."

When I look back at these five names, I don't think any of them intentionally set out to be one of the most influential people in my life. To be blunt, none of them really knew it until I wrote this book. That demonstrates a big point—we can be extremely influential in other people's lives and not even know it.

### DIG-IN TO YOUR OWN SELLING

I challenge you to take three minutes and think of the most influential people in your life. And when you have those three names in mind, I challenge you to call one of them right now and let them know.

Why am I telling you about the top five people who impacted my life? I do so for three reasons:

## 1—To thank them

My life would be tremendously different if I had not interacted with each of them. I am forever grateful they played a part in my life.

## 2—To help you improve your life

A good coach will tell you what you already know, but they tell you at the right time, in the right way, and help you do it while holding you accountable. This causes you to reach higher, dig deeper, and accomplish far more than you could have on your own (to put the tape up on the wall a bit higher). I have had a lot of coaches and mentors, each one of them challenged me to be better.

## 3—To help you get what you want and to be a small piece of influencing someone else's life

You have heard it said that if you help enough people get what they want, you will get what you want. That is especially true in selling, but it is even more true in your life and the impact you make. I want to help you get what you want, but I also hope to motivate you to always reach higher and chase the dreams that are important to you.

Each of us has a curtain, and behind that curtain is what truly motivates us. Being at the top of your sales position is important, and that is important for everyone in sales—but is that what truly motivates you? For me, I want to help others get what they want.

Achieving their personal goals is what helped keep me in the game.

Knowing why you do what you do, knowing what truly motivates you, is vital to your long-term success. My challenge to you is to take what you can from this book, see what you can do, and strive to be one of the five most influential people in someone else's life. I want to be that for others as well. I hope this book may influence you in a way that *How to Win Friends* influenced me.

# 2

# Remember, We All Sell The Same Stuff

*NEED TO ASK you to overlook certain parts of the following story as they may seem crude and possibly vulgar. The overall story is fine, but a particular word in it may be offensive.*

We have all heard it, we have all said it, and yet its use is often frowned upon. I have tried writing this story using different words, but it just doesn't work. So, please forgive me in advance.

Here is the deal—we all poop; dogs dump, cats crap, but chickens shit. Forgive me, but there is no other word for it.

Now, many years ago I sold several tons of chicken shit.

One of my good friends, Kevin Boerboom, had a family farm. It was a farm with about 250,000 chickens.

One cold Saturday, Kevin and I started work at 5 a.m. We both had dates showing up at 6 p.m. at a local restaurant, so we were determined to be there. Without the girls' phone numbers (this was before we had cell phones), it was imperative that we arrive on time. But luck was not on our side. One thing after another went wrong. A manure belt broke, we had a leak in a water line, and the egg conveyor jammed. Every breakdown set us further behind, so we worked faster to catch up, but as soon as we got caught up, something else went wrong.

After a backbreaking twelve-hour day, we finished every chore and were about to get into our cars to drive to town when we remembered we had forgotten to empty the manure spreader behind barn number three. It was November in Minnesota, so we knew it would freeze if we left it until the next morning; it had to be emptied before we left.

I drove Kevin to the back of the barn and left him there. To empty the spreader, Kevin had to drive out to the highway (a fifteen-minute drive) or take a shortcut and go straight through the stream. He asked if he should go around or through it to save time. "Blast through it, but ya gotta hit it hard," I said. He decided to risk it, and you can imagine what happened.

He called me on the radio moments later, explaining he was stuck, and I said I would get the other tractor to pull him out. Thinking we still had a chance to be on time for our dates, I arrived minutes later, and yes, I got my tractor stuck, too. In fact, my tractor was more stuck than his. Kevin then called his dad and asked if he could bring in the big tractor to pull us both out.

Two hours later, both tractors were unstuck, and the manure was spread. Needless to say, we stood up our dates. Our plans were shot to pieces. Our day was horrible.

Later that evening, as we were sitting around having a beer, someone mentioned that if we could dry out the manure, it would be a lot easier to deal with. What a great idea.

A few months later, I was back at NDSU (North Dakota

State University) with Kevin as my roommate when Kevin's dad called. He wanted to know if Kevin and I wanted to head south for a socializing job over spring break.

"As long as it's south, count me in," I replied.

I had not yet learned the importance of getting all the details and hearing what was said versus what I wanted to hear. When he said, "Head south," my mind jumped to Florida or Texas. It may have had something to do with being in North Dakota in late winter, as everything was "south," and everything was warmer than we were. And when he said, "Socialize," I heard, "Party."

Later I got all the details: "Head south" meant a couple of hours south to Sioux Falls, South Dakota. And "socialize" meant we would be talking to a bunch of certified organic farmers at their annual convention.

This was not the spring break I had in mind when I agreed to go. I did not know that Kevin's dad had acted on the drying-out-the-manure idea months earlier. He had figured out a way to dry and pelletize it. He wanted us to sell it as a fertilizer at the certified organic farmers convention. He knew I had spent a few summers selling books door-to-door with Southwestern Advantage, so he figured I could help with sales.

Preparing for our big "spring break" trip, we made up a company name, ordered business cards to match, and did our best to learn as much as possible about fertilizer and organic farming. (Yes, it is safe to say we basically made up the business cards because neither of us knew anything about organic farming.)

We arrived and set up our table with our business cards and several jars of our dried, pelletized manure.

As we were getting organized, I noticed a guy sitting diagonally across and down a bit from us who had what looked like a remarkably similar product. Now anyone who knows me knows

I am not afraid of confrontation, not that this would be confrontational, but this guy was competing with me.

I told Kevin I would be right back as I walked over to check out our competition.

Sure enough, this guy had done the same thing; only he was the real deal. He knew his shit. He knew the nitrogen (N), phosphorus (P), and potassium (K), or NPK for short, value of the dried manure, if it had living matter in it, and that it could be used as a cattle feed supplement. (I still don't even know what that means.) He seemed to know a lot about organic farming.

I waited till a few farmers gathered around his booth and listened as he gave his sales pitch. It was impressive how much he knew about shit.

I was thinking to myself,

> *"Wow, this guy really knows his shit.*
> *Is his shit the same as my shit?*
> *Is his shit better than my shit?*
> *Is there such a thing as good shit?*
> *Is there such a thing as bad shit? Isn't all shit bad?"*

This guy would talk it up with everyone, giving his chicken shit speech, and people would thank him and walk away.

I told Kevin, "We are in deep shit—the guy across from us knows his shit."

Moments later, one of the same farmers who the other guy had just pitched approached our table. He was about to ask a question when Kevin suddenly and conveniently had to go to the bathroom. Walking away, he said over his shoulder, "Ask Joe; he can help you."

I was stuck. I was in a shitty situation. I knew the moment I started talking about my shit, I was in trouble, because I didn't know shit about my shit. I got the guy talking (so I could think of what to say) by peppering him with questions:

"How long have you been farming?

When did you decide to start farming organically? What else?

What made you decide to change?

What has been the biggest problem you have encountered?

What would you do differently?

Can you tell me more about that?

What was the most unexpected thing that has happened since you started?

What else?"

On and on I went with my questions. He would answer one, and I would ask a follow-up, dig-in question about his answer, and he kept talking.

Finally, he said, "I reckon-I think-I might-like to-not-better-oughta-like-try you out."

To this day, I am still not sure what that meant, but I took it as, "Yes, I'd like to place an order with you now."

I replied, "Well, would you like a full load or half-semi load, and where do you want it shipped, to your farm or right to a field?"

"That depends on how much it is," he answered.

For some reason, we had never talked about the price of the product with Kevin's dad, so I completely made up the number. "It's $650 for a full load, and we need half now and the rest on delivery. I will need your address. Do you get your mail at your home or the post office?"

And he gave me his address and wrote out the check.

## WE ALL SELL THE SAME THING

What I learned that day changed how I approach sales. Here is the moral of the story:

> We all sell the same shit.
> We really do.

When it comes to chicken shit, there is no difference between it and anyone else's shit. When it comes to what you sell and what your competitors sell, there really is no difference.

This is a broad statement, but in the consumers' minds, they can go up ten floors or down ten blocks and find someone who sells what you sell. Yes, there are differences, but at the end of the day, from their perspective—it's the same shit. That being the case, I will not compete against their shit. It's rare for me to compete against someone's product. However, I will compete against the other salesperson—and *that* is where you need to focus.

No one can compete against me when I am selling myself; they will lose. And no one can compete against you when you are selling yourself, either.

If you are selling purely on the product, someone is always going to come in with something faster, better, stronger, or cheaper, and they will get the sale.

Always remember: If you win business on price, you will lose it on price.

If you are selling on emotion, relationships, and who you are, nobody is going to beat you. But you are beatable when you sell the same thing as the other salesperson.

Consider this: If you win on relationship, your relationship will help keep the business.

For example, I was doing training in Gulf Shores, Alabama,

with a group of salespeople when we started talking about the benefits of being different. They all agreed and gave reasons such as:

1. Different helps differentiate us from the competition.

2. Different is not boring.

3. Different allows us to offer a new value proposition.

These are all solid reasons for being different.

## DIG-IN TO YOUR OWN SELLING

No one can compete against you when you are selling yourself.

I then asked them to give me their sales pitch, but as soon as they started, I quickly realized we were back at the organic farmers convention—where everyone was selling the same shit.

All these experienced and qualified sales associates who wanted to be different were carbon copies of their competition. The logo, the name, or the color might be different, but it's all the same stuff.

Over the years, I have tried to pull out what's different between salespeople and after talking, making more than 30,000 sales calls, training, and conducting countless sales audits, I end up at the exact same place.

Almost everyone (about 96 percent of the time) in sales starts talking and bragging about their company and how good and great it is. It then shifts to talking about how they are different than everyone else (which they aren't), and finally they talk about their individual experiences. Maybe they mix up the order a bit, but that's about it.

Think back to a previous sales job. Don't you kind of say the same thing today you said back then? After all, isn't that what everyone else is doing?

There have been a few times when I hear a slightly different pitch. It's usually from top producers who step back and ask some original questions, but before long they are back to the usual selling—and talking about how good and great they are.

Sure, it's good to be different than everyone else, and everyone agrees being different is a good thing, yet we are walking down the road running our sales calls just like everyone else.

As I have said many times, we all sell the same shit. And what's more, we sell the same shit the same way. So, in order to get different results, you need to do and think differently.

## PART II

# HOW NOT TO SELL

# 3

# Emotional Selling

L ET'S IMAGINE YOU are a salesperson and have a great meeting with a client. We'll call him Monty.

Let's say it was one of those perfect meetings.

As Monty walks down the hall to meet you, you see he is talking, walking, and joking with a neighbor, who just happens to be there too, and you quickly and naturally join in their conversation. From the get-go, you establish rapport.

Moments later, while you are talking about the trophy fish on his office wall, you notice your best friend from high school is in one of his golf pictures. You also talk about that, and your rapport is boosted even more.

You continue with your pitch, and near the end, you are both excited; he is asking questions, leaning forward, and laughing at your jokes. You even discuss taking the next step forward at another two-week meeting. As you leave his office, the two of you are practically high-fiving each other.

You could say it was a warm and fuzzy meeting, like a Norman Rockwell painting with a cozy fire in the fireplace and a dog sitting in your lap. This meeting was a nine or ten on a scale of one to ten. It could not have gone better.

Two weeks later, as you are getting ready for the second meeting (the follow-up), you see you have a new voicemail. It's Monty and he says, "Hey, I've got to work from home today because I've got a kid who's sick. Sorry, but let's get together again in two weeks. Same time works for me. I'll just plan on seeing you then unless I hear from you. Thanks, Buddy."

You think, "That's okay. We're still good. We've got a definite meeting, just pushed back a bit. He likes me, he called me 'Buddy.' We're good."

Another two weeks go by.

As you get ready for your meeting with Monty, you see another voicemail from him. "Hey, sorry, now I'm sick this week. We need to put it out another two weeks. Shoot, I'm on vacation in two weeks. Tell you what, please call my assistant and set up a time."

You call Monty's assistant and agree on a time and date for your second meeting.

It has been two months since the first meeting, and you get ready for your meeting by reviewing your notes, getting all your details ready, and remembering how fantastic your first meeting was. You remember your neighbor was there and how you both knew your high school buddy.

You arrive at his office right on time and his assistant walks you down the hall. You knock on Monty's open door, and he says, "Come on in. Grab a seat. I've got to finish this email."

It's an awkward silence as he taps away on his keyboard. Finally, he turns to you and says, "Two quick things. First, I got called to a meeting across town, so we may have to cut this a bit short. Second, let's see what you got."

You are ready. You quickly show him the follow-up work on the deal you had discussed in your first meeting. But as you start to go through your proposal, you notice the warm, fuzzy feeling you had during that first meeting is gone. Monty is different. He's looking at his watch and then at his computer. He is not laughing at your jokes or smiling at all. His arms are crossed as if he is closed off to you.

When you are done, Monty says, "You know what? I liked it, but I just need to think about it. Call me back in a month."

You walk out of his office not knowing where you stand with him. On the "great meeting" scale, you went from a nine or ten to maybe a two or three.

A month later, you call him as he had requested, but he replies, "Oh, I didn't get a chance to go over it, so give me another month, okay? Tell you what, call me back next quarter."

And it never ends. You never get back in to see him; the only feedback is, "He said he needs to think about it."

## PUTTING ON THE BRAKES

What happened? How did things digress from such a great initial meeting to a completely flat one the next? How did you lose a sure sale that looked so promising based on your evident camaraderie and interaction?

It just doesn't make sense. How could everything that felt so perfect at the initial meeting with Monty have drained out by the time you had the second meeting?

Most people wonder what went wrong at the second meeting, where did it mess up. I suggest the problem occurred at the first meeting and you are now dealing with it in the second. The reason is that most salespeople approach sales through logic rather than emotion.

Before the word "emotion" throws you off, let me explain why emotion in selling is important. In fact, it's completely natural and will reap you much better results than logical selling. And since one is far more effective than the other, it's worth hearing me out, isn't it?

Let me paint you a picture. It will help with the explanation and understanding.

There are two parts to every sale, two "buckets," I like to say, that need to be filled. They are:

1. The logical sale (logical bucket)

2. The emotional sale (emotional bucket)

The main difference between the two is that a logical sale is filled up with your voice, you are the expert, while the emotional bucket is filled with their voice.

It looks like this:

**LOGICAL SALE:**

Bucket with *your* voice, your words in it

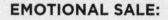

**EMOTIONAL SALE:**

Bucket with *their* voice, their words in it

Look at what comes out of most marketing departments. It's usually logical.

Both parts of a sale, both buckets, are certainly important, but an emotional sale makes things happen. That is because emotions compel us to act, whereas logic typically does not. Logic reinforces what we decide but it doesn't help us act or decide.

In your career as a salesperson, odds are you have offered the lowest price to a prospect, only to see that the prospect purchased from your competitor whose prices were higher than yours, correct?

We all have experienced that, but what causes such a thing to happen? After all, your discounted price was clearly better than your competitor's. Logically, the prospect should have bought from you.

The reason your competitor got the sale is:

- Because of the relationship they had with your prospect,
- And relationships involve emotions,
- All things being equal, emotions will outsell logic most of the time.

A logical sale is important because it confirms the sale down the road, but if you don't make that emotional sale on the front end, there is nothing to confirm.

## WHAT MAKES EMOTIONAL SELLING WORK

How do you make an emotional sale? How do you go about making a sale based on emotion?

First, recognize that a logical sale is driven by math. Your voice tells them the logical reasons why they would benefit from your offer.

This is not bad. Both logic and your voice have their place, but emotional selling is driven by emotion, and most importantly, their voice.

Let me say that again, your voice fills the logical bucket, or makes the logical sale.

Their voice fills the emotional bucket, or makes the emotional sale. When they are doing the talking, they are selling themselves. They are filling their emotional bucket.

Let's say you are a financial advisor working with your client, a businessperson, on his retirement plan. He says he wants to have a certain amount of money in retirement by the time he retires, so you estimate how many years he will be in retirement, calculate how many years until he retires, and figure out how much he needs to save per year to reach that goal.

It's a number. It's math. And you can't argue with math.

Most of us in sales are experts on making that type of logical sale. Entire marketing departments exist to provide their salespeople with every resource imaginable to answer those types of questions, calculations, and estimations.

When all is said and done, it's your voice that delivers the logical solution to your prospects.

But here is the problem with logic: logic is finite. You can use only so much logic, and once you have stated the logical points, you have nowhere else to go. How often does the retiring businessperson need to hear how much he should save each month? One time is probably enough.

### DIG-IN TO YOUR OWN SELLING

Whoever is talking is buying.
If you are talking more than your prospects,
then you are buying their objections. But if
they are talking more than you, then they are
buying whatever it is you are selling.

## THINK OF THE BUCKETS

Back to the bucket analogy; imagine you have a bucket that is full of water. It's full, right to the brim. If you add any more water, it will spill over the edge, be wasted, and make a mess.

The same is true about a logical sale. Once someone is logically sold, you can't sell any more logic. If you do, it's wasteful, messy, and probably a little bit annoying.

That makes sense, right? It's simply a matter of volume. The bucket is full. You cannot add more.

But emotions are not finite like logic. Rather, emotions are infinite, goofy, and unpredictable. They don't make sense. They change all the time.

What's more, the emotional bucket has holes in it. Emotions are fickle. They can change, they often do, and for no reason.

Remember the engagement with Monty that went from an awesome warm-and-fuzzy first meeting to a flat-and-dead second meeting? Though the first meeting was amazing, by the second meeting, his emotional bucket was almost empty.

The first meeting with my neighbor and my high school buddy had nothing to do with logical selling. It only helped fill Monty's emotional bucket.

From that perspective, what he said and how he responded at the second meeting makes much more sense. When he asked, "What do you got?" giving a logical answer was filling a bucket that was already full.

As a result:

- He wasn't engaged.

- He didn't like you as much.

- It felt transactional—for both of us.

- You were repeatedly put off.

- It wasn't fun—it actually sucked.

- Nothing clicked.

Every emotional bucket has holes in it; all your emotional connections and camaraderie—no matter how warm and fuzzy it felt—had drained out.

Looking back, because the meetings with Monty were real, I realize his pushback put me on the defensive.

My response was to inaccurately try to refill the logic bucket rather than the emotional bucket. I jumped right into my all logic offer, and he didn't need that.

It was of no value and probably annoyed him. In fact, it makes complete sense. Remember what he did:

- He looked at his watch.

- He looked at his computer.

- He crossed his arms.

- He didn't act.

He then shut it down when he responded to my reselling with logic: "You know what, I liked it, but I just need to think about it. Call me back in a month."

From this experience, I learned never to present any solutions, not to offer logic, or try to sell logically, until *after* I check on the level of the emotional bucket.

That is what I should have done with Monty.

Is the emotional bucket empty? How full is it? Do you even know? How can you tell?

Take a minute and look at your pipeline, or more specifically, how many good deals are open with prospective clients who are saying, "Let me think about it." They are all logically sold, which means they are just half sold. Their emotional bucket needs to be filled.

We will get more into the details of checking on the emotional bucket levels and how to sell emotionally, but it is important right now to understand why emotional selling is important.

It is important because it is required. It is the spark of the sale. Emotions cause people to act.

The emotional bucket has holes in it. Whatever is in it will leak out, and it leaks constantly.

That makes sense because our emotions are constantly changing. If you are only selling with logic, you are missing the most important bucket. And if you are not continually selling emotionally, that bucket is draining out.

In short, you need to repeatedly sell the same customer emotionally and check the depth of their emotional bucket. It's not because you did a bad job the first time, but because emotions leak out of buckets. Emotions change. They just do.

When you refill and refill that emotional bucket, you are increasing the odds that you will be the salesperson who benefits from the sale, the referral, the repeat business, and the word-of-mouth marketing.

It's all based on emotional selling and the relationship you establish during the sale.

It is important to note that there is a point where trust comes into play with the emotional bucket. Most salespeople have a few clients they have "control over," who "trust" them, and that is ideally what we are all looking for.

The more trust you have, the deeper your relationship, the faster their emotional bucket will fill up.

Trust is something that is built over time. It forms at the bottom of the emotional bucket, keeping the emotions from leaking out quite so quickly, filling the holes—not all of them, but most.

## DIG-IN TO YOUR OWN SELLING

Trust is what helps keep emotions from leaking
out of the emotional bucket.

## THE EMOTIONAL BUCKET
## NEEDS TO BE REFILLED

The first meeting with prospects is often warm and fuzzy because you are excited to meet one another. But the excitement wears off. The emotional buckets need to be refilled.

At the start of this chapter with Monty, I chatted and joked about our neighbor and mutual friend, and he filled up his emotional bucket by telling stories about our friend.

He was all excited, yet none of it had anything to do with the sale. That's all fine, as you make an emotional sale first.

But when you show up for your scheduled appointment months later, you must know your prospect's emotional bucket is empty. The warm and fuzzy encounter from your first meeting has passed and you can't start telling stories about your friend again. It doesn't work that way.

*Their emotional bucket needs to be refilled, but not with what filled it the first time.* You must figure out another way.

You can bring up whatever it was that was talked about previously and ask them more about it. Merely repeating what they said before probably won't work, so get them talking. It is imperative at this point that their voice refills their emotional bucket.

When you are selling, always keep a mental eye on that emotional bucket. *Always look for* what *they want and* why *they want it.* In all they say, you want them to tell you *why.* Getting them to talk about their *why* is the fastest and surest way to fill up their emotional bucket.

I strive to never sell, teach, coach, train, or speak until I have created space to have that conversation. Or I make sure they are emotionally engaged, so their bucket can be filled.

Their voice saying why they want something is what fills up their emotional bucket. And that enhances or adds to your relationship.

Remember, as a salesperson, your voice fills up the logical bucket, while your prospect's voice fills up their emotional bucket.

## MAKE THIS PRACTICAL

Over the years, I've learned to ask a lot of prospects questions centered on what they they want and why they want what they want.

The *what* is important, but the *why* taps into their own motivations, dreams, and emotions. You want to get your prospects talking, and more specifically, get them talking about their *whys*.

Asking these types of questions may seem silly at first, even a bit awkward, but it is extremely important. Often, you may find that they don't have an answer, and that's okay. It gets them thinking. If they are thinking, they are engaged. The more they can refine their focus, the better. It causes them to act.

Practice this approach, then use it with your prospects. When talking with a prospect, here is what it could sound like:

> "A lot of our competitors start by asking you *what* you want and following up with details. It is important to do that, but I strive to have you tell me *why* you want it. That is important to me because it helps me build your plan. More importantly, you saying what you want, why you want it and, why it is important to you crystalizes your thinking and helps you clarify your goals."

It's similar to this: You set the goal of going to Europe for the summer. You spend time working on travel options, visas, things to see, weather, mountain climbing, what to wear, etc. You get all that stuff figured out and you are set to leave tomorrow morning when it hits you—you really want to go to Peoria, Illinois.

That's what can happen if you are not clear and have not verbally said what you want and why you want it. Again, I know it may seem silly to ask *why* questions, but it's necessary.

You are asking for your prospect's permission (both now and going forward) to ask them why questions randomly and periodically to ensure they get where they want to go. You are literally asking for permission to fill the emotional bucket or, more importantly, make the emotional sale.

## THE EMOTIONAL SALE

How to sell nothing is a logical way to make the emotional sale. Take a look at the following graph called The Buying Curve:

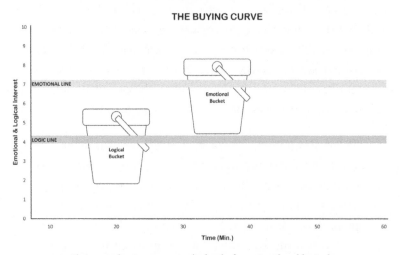

The vertical axis represents the level of emotional and logical interest. The horizontal line represents increments of time.

The Buying Curve simply demonstrates that things have to make sense logically and emotionally and may happen at different times. We, as buyers, will not move forward unless it makes logical sense. The logical bucket needs to be filled in order even to consider the next step.

The emotional bucket is a bit higher on the engagement line, meaning we need their emotional buy-in, for them to act.

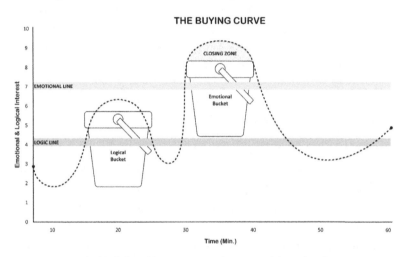

The black dotted line represents the prospect's logical and emotional interest level as we move through the sale.

In this Buying Curve, the prospect starts at a "3" in engagement interest. A common mistake that salespeople make is they start with a show-up, throw-up presentation. This is where they brag about how good, how great, or how wonderful they are. This causes the prospect to be less engaged and it works against you.

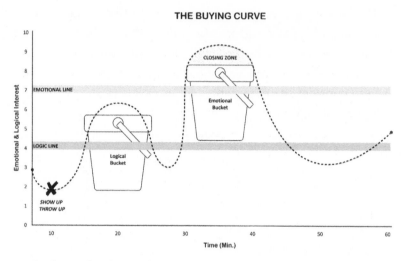

The logical sale is when we start asking questions about their current reality: what they have now, how it works, how long they have had it, etc. It is your data gathering or factfinding. That bucket is filled with the salesperson's voice. You make the logical sale.

Here, another common mistake happens. You think that they are sold with logic and you close too soon. Odds are, you will get a no or "I need to think about it."

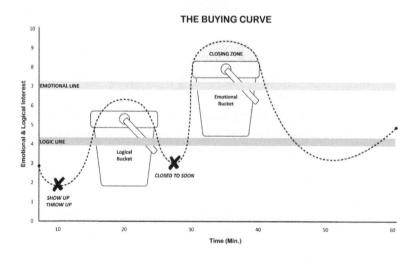

The prospect will not move forward unless you get them above the emotional buying line or allow their voice to fill their emotional bucket.

Once the dotted line crosses the emotional line, you should close—this is your closing zone. If you wait too long to close, you simply allow them to drop below the closing line. You have just talked past the close or talked yourself out of a sale. This is the most common sales mistake.

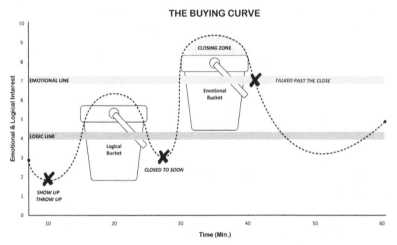

Remember, *Whoever is talking is buying.* The emotional bucket is filled with their voice. Your voice fills the logical bucket.

Because selling is a process, the prospect needs to become emotionally bought in somewhere on that continuum. No decisions will happen until this happens and they're engaged above the buying line.

So, for your prospect to purchase, you must first bring them to the logic line and then forward in time to the emotional line. *Getting their interest level above both lines is important.* Logic confirms the sale but does not complete the sale in the prospect's mind.

Crossing the emotional line means the prospect is bought in emotionally and ready to move toward the close.

Both buckets need to remain full to move to the next step when we're selling.

The logical bucket tends to stay full once filled. Remember, if you have a bucket full of water and you try to put more water into it, you can't. It will just overflow and make an annoying mess. I have often seen this drain the emotional bucket—no one likes to be annoyed. So, as a warning, when the logic bucket is full, it is very important not to continue selling logic.

The emotional bucket is different. It has holes and does not stay full. Emotions change because they're weird and fickle. *The essence of selling nothing is keeping the emotional bucket full long enough for the sale to be made and closed.*

We can have the prospect emotionally engaged with us at one meeting, then the emotions change over time. We will not get them to act until we get them emotionally engaged and back above the buying line again.

## THE E.A.R.N.I.N.G. SALE SYSTEM

I bet most, if not all, salespeople have a plan as to how a sale should go. Sales plans are like battle plans, where you can throw the plans out the window once they start. That is why I created the E.A.R.N.I.N.G. Sale System. A simple acronym to help keep your sales or battle plans on track.

In The Buying Curve below, you'll see that the E.A.R.N.I.N.G. Sale System comes into play at the very beginning of the sale because we must earn the right to ask for their business to get across the logic line, also known as the buying line.

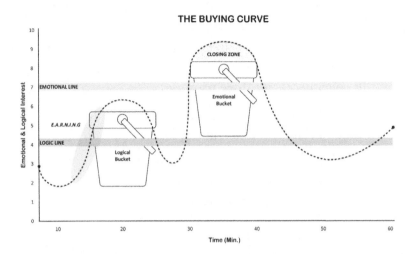

**THE BUYING CURVE**

*E: Evaluate.* Evaluate their current reality. This is the equivalent of being a factfinder. You are a data gatherer, and to get enough data to learn about your prospect's needs, you must ask enough questions. You need to know what product or service they already have. Then you must determine whether you will show them a similar, new, or completely different product. If you are selling a similar product or service, or making an apples-to-apples comparison, you must ask enough questions to know what type of apples they have. Same goes for a new product or service (an apples-to-oranges comparison), you still must ask enough questions to know what type of apples they have.

*A: Advantages.* Ask about the advantages of what they have right now. Why does it work for them? What do they like about it? What do they like about what they are doing now? Believe it or not, these questions don't make prospects stay where they are. Often, I get push-back from my clients who say, "Joe, I am not comfortable asking that. I feel like I'm talking them into keeping what they already have." These questions play to your success for three reasons:

1. Few salespeople ask these questions, so it differentiates you. I get different results because I do different things.

2. It screams confidence, and they respect that, which makes your stock level go up.

3. When they start telling you why they like what they have, they are literally telling you their own hot buttons. You may hear, "My current vendor is really good with customer service," or "She is very organized," or "I like how they keep me in the loop." Whatever they say, I am thinking, "Ding, ding, ding, I have to close on that in either five minutes, five weeks, or five months."

   Whatever you hear is important to your prospects, and you know exactly what to do to win their business. Whatever they say they like, you need to sell *that*.

*R: Revise.* Revise what they have or what they are currently doing that needs to change. You need to know what they want to do differently. What needs to be fixed. This is the major reason they will take the next step with you. I don't lead off with this, but it is a big piece. The fact that you are sitting there in front of them shows they have a real need. I personally believe that in today's busy, fast-paced world, if people are "sitting" with me and having a conversation about what I sell, they have a need for Executive Level Coaching, consulting or speaking. We are too busy to sit and hear about something we may need. I will also admit that it may be an internalized self-talking affirmation I now 100 percent believe.

*N: No.* Who can say "no" to your offer? Who can say "yes" to it? Who else needs to be there? Who writes the check? You need to know who the decision-makers are. The answers to these questions tell you if the prospect you are talking to has the authority to make decisions or write the checks.

If not, you may need to step back. It is very frustrating to do a presentation and then be told, "I have to check with so-and-so."

At the very least, you must redo your presentation for that decision-maker.

Also, if this nondecision-maker tries to go back and sell the real decision-maker, it never works. They are not an expert on your product or service, so they can't sell your product or service; they are not an expert on you, so they can't sell you. You must learn who can say "yes" or "no" to your deal and work only with that prospect. Sometimes, I will stop the meeting, stop the pitch, and try to shift the focus by setting up a meeting with the decision-maker. Sometimes I can and sometimes I can't. However, it is extremely rare for me to go over pricing if I am not with the decision-maker. I will wait.

*I: Interpret.* Interpret back what they just said. Most of us listen so we can respond, and we get so busy figuring out our answer or what we will say next that we don't listen to what they say. It is so much better to sit and listen, then repeat back what they said. This one little step has a huge impact. In fact, this is a big, big piece of selling nothing. If you were to take one piece and apply it tomorrow, you would see how it changes the entire conversation. I dare you to try it tomorrow and shoot me a note about how it worked. Go to www.sellnothing.co and visit my Success Page or scan the QR code below to share your stories or successes.

When I interpret back what they just said, in a sense I am selling nothing. When repeating back what the prospects say, the following things happen:

1. It shows that you listened to them.

2. It shows that they are important.

3. It shows that you are on their side.

4. It confirms their thinking in their own minds.

5. It creates a buying atmosphere.

6. It helped prospects to like you a bit more.

7. It removes all the "pressure close" out of the room.

8. It shows that you understand them.

After all, prospects' biggest complaint is, "Nobody listens to me." Your goal is to get them to say, "Wow, you said it better than I did!" At that point, you have moved them mentally. They know you get them, and this is a strong emotional connection, which helps fill their emotional bucket (using their voice and repeating their words helps to fill their bucket). Again, this is a huge step because it makes them feel like you are on their side of the table, and you haven't even started selling yet—what a great spot to be in.

*N: Nothing.* What will happen if they do nothing, or nothing changes? That's a great question to ask because it establishes a sense of urgency. It's a tough question and may even be a little awkward. Ask it, then let them sit and think about it for a while. Allowing them to stay comfortable means nothing will change; outside of the comfort zone is where growth occurs.

It is quite common for prospects to give short and sweet answers. You want more than that, so learn to ask, "What else?" A lot. You want them to think, "I just answered that; now I have to really think about it." You want them a tad annoyed, to wallow in their discomfort, because those emotions also help fill their emotional bucket.

*G: Gain.* What do they have to gain? What is the value of making a change? What would it be like if this issue was put to bed? What could they do if it was resolved? This is where you set the table for selling your product or services.

To reiterate the above, we're asking the prospects all of these questions in the E.A.R.N.I.N.G. Sale System because it begins to fill the logical bucket and take them above the logic line.

For a free printable version of the E.A.R.N.I.N.G. Sale System, visit www.convertsalesfaster.com.

> ## DIG-IN TO YOUR OWN SELLING
>
> Have you planned a sales pitch, know what you want to say, know when to say it, and are confident in your plan, only to get into the meeting and your client takes you off track? That's sales. Acronyms help you get on track.

## HOW DO YOU GET PROSPECTS TO FILL UP THEIR EMOTIONAL BUCKET?

If we go back to the chicken shit story—I didn't know it then, but I kept him talking by asking "dig-in" questions. The definition of a "dig-in" question is getting prospects to tell me why it is important. It's the why behind their what. Dig-in questions fill their emotional bucket. I strive never to start selling until I have heard them tell me their whys. It needs to be said by them; the power is in their voice, not mine.

Examples of dig-in questions are:

*Can you tell me more?*

*What does that look like?*

*When you say _____, what do you mean by that?*

*Can you give me an example?*

*Can you say that again?*

*What else?*

Every answer fills their emotional bucket. You can ask dig-in question followed by dig-in question followed by dig-in question. They are telling you their why. Just sell that. I will close on that in five minutes, five weeks, or five months.

It puts you in a position to sell what they want to buy versus selling what you want to sell.

Dig-in questions are helpful throughout the conversation, but they are to be married to and embedded with the E.A.R.N.I.N.G. Sale System. Dig-in questions fill their emotional bucket.

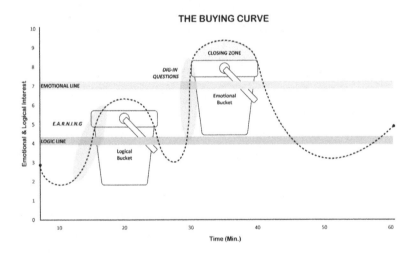

Although it's shown in The Buying Curve that both the E.A.R.N.I.N.G. Sale System and dig-in questions occur at separate times, they can and should happen at the same time.

For a free printable version of the E.A.R.N.I.N.G. Sale System, visit www.convertsalesfaster.com.

# 4

# Show Up, Throw Up

YOU ALREADY KNOW from experience that when you go to see a doctor, you will probably get a few minutes of actual time together to diagnose your problem.

I once had a gig with a startup that sold onsite clinics to schools. As a result, I spent a lot of time with doctors. In fact, one doctor told me that most doctors only have three to five minutes to spend with each patient before they need to move on.

Regardless of how much time they have with you, it only makes sense for you to use that time wisely, correct? A lot needs to happen and there is no time to waste. That time is critical and must be used wisely. If not, the patient loses.

Let's say you have a splitting headache and go visit your doctor. It's your first visit to this doctor because he is a specialist and you were referred to him.

After sitting in the waiting room for ten minutes, you are taken back to a smaller room where you wait alone for another twenty to thirty minutes.

Finally, the door opens and your doctor steps into the room, shakes your hand, and introduces himself. Then he:

- Points to a picture on the wall, saying, "Here is where I did my undergrad."

- Points to a framed diploma and says, "I went to medical school here."

- Shows you a graph and says, "Here is a list of my patients for the last two years with their BMI (body mass index)."

- Lists all the charitable organizations he is involved with and says, "We raised over a million dollars for charity last year."

- Gushes about the new state-of-the-art maternity ward they will be building next year.

He then looks at his watch. "Oh, I have about a minute left!" he exclaims. "You are having headaches I see. Why don't you take two aspirin and come back and see me in a week?"

How much confidence will you have in his prescription based on his utter lack of diagnosis? Probably zero.

The fact is, your doctor can't fix you until you tell him how and why.

And here is my point:

*You can't sell anyone until they tell you how and why.*

What you would have preferred is your doctor asking you questions that might help you:

- How long has this been going on?
- Do you get headaches at the same time each day?
- How are you sleeping?
- Are some headaches worse than others?
- What's going on at home—any new changes?
- How about work?
- How have you been eating?

Again, your doctor can't fix you until you tell them how and why.

In all honesty, do you really care about where your doctor went to school, did their undergrad work, sends charitable money, or what's up with the new maternity ward? (You do have a headache, after all.)

Personally, I have four kids, and I never want to see the inside of a maternity ward again.

Here is a quick test: Do you even know where your doctor went to school? Or your dentist? Or your CPA? Or your realtor? Do you really care?

That doctor did the famous "show up, throw up" talk in sales. It happens in every industry, all the time.

How often do we brag about how good we are? About how our company does this better than anyone else? Or about an award we won or a bonus trip we went on?

Whenever we focus on what we can do, we monopolize the conversation. And every time we do that, we lose. We are filling that logical bucket, but that is not the sale that needs to be made now.

The prospect starts out with some interest and gives you time to pitch the sale. If you spend most of this time talking, you are throwing up on your prospects and seeing what sticks. You will never get to the buying line this way because nobody likes that. Eventually, the customer walks away, and the sale is lost.

Again, the fact is, *whoever is talking is buying.* And if you are doing most of the talking, then you are buying their objections. You are buying their limitations. You are buying their reasons to say "no." You may even keep them below the logic line because they stop listening. Neither bucket will get filled by showing up and throwing up.

But if your prospects are talking, they are buying whatever you are selling.

## NATURAL KICKBACK

Back to the doctor who rambled on and on about himself and failed to listen to you—what is your reaction to a doctor like that?

I've heard people say about this type of doctor:

- He's a jerk.

- It's all about him.

- He's arrogant and proud, and that turns me off.

- I'd never go back to him.

- I would tell my friends to avoid him.

Any doctor who does a show-up, throw-up presentation will naturally get blowback. We don't like to be treated that way.

Would you take their advice? Would you take their prescription?

What we want is for him to address our real needs, to ask questions, and to focus on helping us.

But doctors who ask us questions force us to answer in our own words. Our voice fills our emotional bucket, the same emotional bucket that causes us to act to take their prescription.

We really don't care about what's important to him—unless that helps us.

## DIG-IN TO YOUR OWN SELLING

Doctors can't fix you until you tell them how or why. And we can't sell to anyone until they tell us how or why.

Did you catch that? We don't care about what he is talking about. Everything in his show-up, throw-up talk could have been eliminated, and you would have probably said:

- He's nice.

- It was about me.

- He's humble, and I like that.

- I'll go back to him.

- I will tell my friends to see him.

Wow, the exact opposite. Doctors can't fix you until you tell them how and why they must fix you. And the same directly applies to us as salespeople.

*We can't sell to anyone until they tell us how and why to sell to them.*

Below is an example of how to skip over the show-up, throw-up part. It is one of my favorite things to say to a new prospect after establishing rapport. I say this at the beginning of *every* new conversation:

"Is it okay if I skip over the part where I brag about myself and how good and great I am?"

I love saying that. It gets them laughing, and they always say, "Yes." And I proceed to start asking them questions. I start the E.A.R.N.I.N.G. piece and sprinkle in dig-in questions.

Interestingly enough, they never go back and ask me to brag about myself.

That screams confidence. I don't need to brag. I'm good and this isn't about me. That is powerful.

Many salespeople will show up and throw up at the beginning of their sales call without knowing that a selling cycle or process should be followed. If you were to Google "selling cycle," you would find there are many variations and steps. I prefer following the 7-Step Selling Cycle shown here:

## THE 7-STEP SELLING CYCLE

**STEP 1:**
Data Gather

**STEP 2:**
First Contact

**STEP 3:**
Foundation

**STEP 4:**
Pitch

**STEP 5:**
Answer Objections

**STEP 6:**
Close

**STEP 7:**
Ask for Referrals

Each step follows the other, assuming this is a one-call close sale. This cycle is repeated or partially repeated for longer selling cycles. In other words, I use this framework in every interaction for longer selling cycles.

## Step 1: Data Gather

In the pre-approach, gather as much information as possible before seeing your prospects. Go online and collect general contact information, research their industry, and details about their company. Look hard to find a *silver bullet,* which is a piece of interesting information you know that the average Joe on the street does not know.

## Step 2: First Contact

Once you know more about your prospect, move to the approach or first contact, which is your connection. Maybe you will speak on the phone, via Zoom, or face-to-face. This is where we use the silver bullets.

## Step 3: Foundation

Foundations are incredibly important because everything is built on them. What happens first in building a relationship is where the sale is made. Weak foundations cause buildings to fail, and weak sales foundations cause sales to not happen. This is where we are earning the sale and digging in to allow them to fill their emotional bucket.

## Step 4: Pitch

The pitch is your proposal or illustration. This is where you blend the logical and emotional sales, where we sell to their why.

## Step 5: Answer Objections

In this step of the cycle, you answer and overcome objections anticipated in advance.

## Step 6: Close

The close is where you agree to the next step.

## Step 7: Ask For Referrals

Here is where you ask for referrals and go back to the data gather.

Ideally the 7-Step Selling Cycle is a perfect loop, but the steps may be applied out of order, all at once, and repeatedly. Do whatever it takes. Just be flexible and confident because you understand the loop. You know where you are going and that good results are coming.

# PART III

# WHERE THE SALE REALLY STARTS

# 5

# Step 1: Data Gather

IN TODAY'S DIGITAL world, a name and phone number just aren't enough. Salespeople often complain they have names and numbers for referrals, but they can't get in touch with anyone, or they leave a message and don't hear back. This is especially true with our high-end prospects.

The solution? It's what I call a silver bullet. A silver bullet is a personal bit of information that an average Joe on the street doesn't know. You get it by asking your prospects or clients specific questions about their referrals as they are giving them to you. It is your ticket to an open door and starts building a relationship.

When you are getting referrals (the last step in The 7-Step Selling Cycle,) begin by asking a few fluff questions, such as:

- How long have you known (the name of the referral)?

- How long have they worked there?

- What do they do for work?

Questions like these are good information and natural questions you want to ask. They fit, and that leads to what you really need to know. Most salespeople stop there and miss the most important part.

Once you have them in a "question-answer mode," get to the real questions, where you get the silver bullets:

- Hey, I'm simply curious. What type of decision-maker are they? Are they a type-A person? A talker? Or a numbers person?

- What do you respect most about (the name of the referral)?

- Tell me a funny story about him/her. Why would you mention their name?

- I was just wondering, why do you think I should call them?

Then be quiet.

Listen.

And take notes.

It is incredibly valuable to ask these types of questions, but you can't lead off with them. You first need to get them used to what you are doing. Then hit them with your questions that net your silver bullets.

Having as many silver bullets as you can collect is incredibly important. These valuable nuggets of information can be used on phone calls, left on voicemails, and used during face-to-face meetings.

When you are getting referrals, your questions need to be laser-beam focused on getting those silver bullets. Here are real examples of silver bullets I received from a client who gave me two referrals:

*Silver Bullets For Mary:*

- At my level, but at a different branch
- Has a very high energy level (You can get tired just being in the same room as her.)
- Is one of the most organized people he knows
- Is a great person
- Everybody likes her
- Went from managing three people to managing fifty

*Silver Bullets For Aaron:*

- Makes good money
- Is not a meathead
- Can drink with the best of them
- Treats people the right way
- Genuinely cares about the people he works with
- Is a great family guy

As you can see, there are a lot of silver bullets in these descriptions about Mary and Aaron. It took time to get them, but it was worth it. Both referrals became clients.

Each silver bullet is valuable, but don't feel pressured to use them all in one sitting. Realistically, you can't, but there is always one that sticks out; use that.

The time to put your silver bullets to work is when you are talking with prospects—during the first contact of the sale or when leaving voicemails. These detailed and specific nuggets of information are perfect because, most likely, you will be sent to voicemail when you call a referral.

When I called Aaron, I ended up in his voicemail. I left a message that said:

> "Hey, Aaron, it's Joe Pallo. Mark Jones mentioned your name the other day. He told me you're not a (slight pause and laugh) meathead. Please call me at 612-805-7576."

If I leave that message, he is going to call me back. Why? He's intrigued. He wonders what else Mark may have said, how I know this, and why I called him.

Often, we will get inside jokes as silver bullets. Take a minute to make sure it is okay for you to share that inside joke about Aaron "not being a meathead." I asked Mark to explain it a bit more; Aaron would laugh, and I'll be in by using an inside joke.

And the phone rings. (Imagine that—having referrals call you.) That is how valuable silver bullets are.

Silver bullets make your referrals so much more than just a name and number. Those are no longer enough, so don't settle for less than one or two silver bullets per referral. Silver bullets allow you to draft off the referee's relationship onto the first contact and boost your relationship.

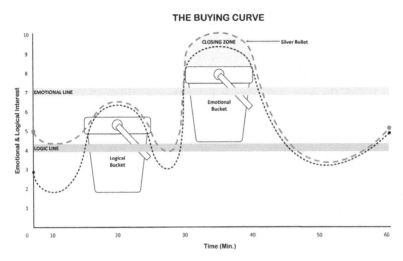

**THE BUYING CURVE**

The more bullets you get, the better. You can use one on your first call and then continue to use them on the second, third, and fourth calls or messages. Mention a different silver bullet in every call or message.

Eventually, the referral *will* call you. With all the bullets I had on Aaron, it was inevitable he would eventually call me. And with him, it took just one silver bullet.

I left one message for him to call me back; he called me back within fifteen minutes, and he became a client and a good friend—but I'm not 100 percent convinced he is not a meathead.

Think of how this enhances your confidence when calling on your prospects. Your thinking is different. You go from "I have to call" to "I get to call." That is a huge boost, and they can hear the confidence in your voice.

Now, when you do leave a voicemail with a silver bullet, they will call you back. And when they do call you back, what should you do?

First, always enter their contact info into your phone to help you identify them and remind you who referred them. Put both names on your contact card, the referee and the referral, and the

73

silver bullets, you want to tie them together because this helps keep you organized.

Second, though this is extremely hard, do not give them your sales pitch right then and there when they call you back.

Why? Because you are not in control of this call. You have no idea what might be happening on the other end of the line. They might be driving, about to go into a movie, or sitting on a plane. You could get most of the way through your pitch and they cut you off.

All that momentum, the power of the meathead silver bullet, is lost.

Partial engagement is not sufficient. You want full engagement. Instead, say something like,

> "Hey Aaron, thanks for calling me back. I was kind of worried that mentioning Mark's name would hurt me more than it helped."

Pause for laughter.

> "I apologize, I wanted to take your call, but I am heading into a meeting myself. Can we set up a time to talk later?"

This does several things:

1. It elevates the importance of your call.

2. It minimizes time limitations.

3. It allows you to focus on selling so you are in the selling mode.

4. It screams confidence and professionalism.

5. It gently puts you in control.

Again, it is hard for a salesperson not to jump into a sales pitch, but it pays to set up your first meeting properly.

**6**

# Step 2: First Contact

C OLD CALLS OR solicitations are a part of sales we all hate, but here we are. The following is the thought process behind the first contact with new prospects.

Do you have a consistent way to talk to new prospects when you call them? Most salespeople say they "kind of do," but they really don't. They just wing it.

When speaking or training on sales talks, I usually get pushback from someone saying, "I can't use a script. I'll sound robotic."

In truth, for every salesperson who makes this objection, many more are thinking it.

Let me tell you—if you work your tail off to get a referral, contact that referral, and months later, when you finally get them on the line and allow yourself to sound robotic… you may be in the wrong career.

A first impression of being passive and robotic would admittedly not be a good look.

But is it true? Does using a script make you sound like a robot? Not at all.

## DIG-IN TO YOUR OWN SELLING

Working from a script is not about "being a robot." It is about being ready to listen to what your prospects are really saying. It means being fully present in your sales calls.

Working from a script does the following:

1. *It allows you to be confident.* If you know what you will say, you will sound more confident.

2. *It keeps you on track.* And if they get you off track, you can get back on track easily.

3. *It allows you to listen.* If you are wondering what you will say next, you aren't listening.

4. *It allows for consistency.* If you and your team say something different each time, you don't know what works, what doesn't, and what to correct.

Sure, you do have to tailor your memorized pitch and personalize it, keeping it somewhat consistent, but it works.

For example, my pitch (which has not changed in twenty-five years) is as follows:

When I call to speak with a prospect, I say: "Hey, Aaron, it's Joe Pallo."

I do *not* say: "Hey, Aaron. This is Joe Pallo."

Why? Because saying "this is" screams, "I'm a salesperson."

Do you call a friend and say, "This is Joe"? Of course not. You would say, "It's Joe," because it's much more familiar and natural. In my pitch, I pause here. I let their mind wonder, "Who the heck is Joe Pallo?" It's good for the person to wonder about that. That is what I want them to be thinking.

Then I say:

"Hey, I don't want you racking your brain trying to figure out who I am. We haven't met yet."

I force myself to chuckle when I say this. It works. It might seem weird to do so, but it forces me to be focused and present on the call. You can't be passive when you are forcing a chuckle. It's intentional, and you want this first impression to be focused, present, and fully intentional.

In addition, I'm saying out loud what the person is thinking. Subconsciously, we all like people who agree with us and think along similar lines.

At that point, I'm only three seconds into the call and already saying what they are thinking. That gets their attention.

Then I pause again and let my prospect begin to wonder why I'm calling. Then I will say:

"Hey, Bill mentioned your name the other day. I'm not sure if mentioning his name's going to help me or hurt me."

Again, I'm saying what they are thinking. This is the second time I'm saying what they're thinking. And I throw in a bit of humor. This helps build rapport, and it helps me figure out the personality type of the person I'm dealing with.

If they get right to the point and say, "Yeah, I know Bill. What do you need?" then I have a fairly clear idea of their personality type. They are a type A person; I need to get to my point right away.

But if they say, "Yeah, I know Bill. He was over at our house this weekend. The kids were over. We played in the pool." Then I know they are a talker. I should let them get their words out.

Their response helps me understand their personality type—no-nonsense, straight to the point, more talkative, open, and easygoing.

Next are the silver bullets. I may say something like,

> "Bill said you're one of the most organized people he knows. What he respects most about you is that you take care of your clients. You go over, above, and beyond. Am I talking to the right guy?"

Now they wonder, "Okay, I like him, but what does he want, and how do I get him off this call?" I want them to think that. I try to wait until they wonder how to get me off the phone.

Then I might say:

> "If I can, I wanted to ask you a few quick questions—your answers will either end the call or get you thinking this may be worth a bit more time."

This is the third time I'm saying what Aaron is thinking. I have their attention. Now I can start my pitch.

I should note you don't want to wait too long for an answer. After a brief pause, start asking your questions. If you wait for them to answer, it will get awkward.

For the record, it has been my experience that about 60 percent of the time they will say, "Go ahead."

With that, I have permission to qualify him. In reality, my questions are the start of him telling me how and why to sell him.

The odds are extremely high at that point, just twenty seconds into it, that I will get a meeting with Aaron.

And that is how I start working with my new leads.

At this point, you have your script, and you know your prospect's personality type. The next step is creating the right environment for your face-to-face or virtual meeting.

## DIG-IN TO YOUR OWN SELLING

Have you ever had meetings where everything goes well, but they just need "to think about it"? If you hear that, think back to your presentation—who did most of the talking? You must have. That's what I would bet. You sold logic, and they didn't buy.

# 7

# Step 3: Foundation

WITH SO MANY important steps in The 7-Step Selling Cycle, clients always want to know which step is the most important.

They are all important, but people who know sales, or those who intuitively know people, will choose laying out the foundation as the most important step in the cycle. And if I had to choose one step, I would agree.

Why? Because the foundation is where the sale really happens. It's where we generate emotion—where the emotional selling process begins and lives.

**DIG-IN TO YOUR OWN SELLING**

The sale is made during the foundation.

There are five cornerstone elements used to build a strong foundation:

1. **Eliminate distractions**
   It's your show. You set the stage for how the meeting will happen. For example, if you are meeting people in their office and building rapport, you want the prospect to know you are serious when you talk about business. So, you stand up and ask permission to close the door. This way, you eliminate all distractions, and it helps you establish control.

2. **Build rapport by using other people's names**
   Using people's names is not flaunting or an egotistical name-dropping moment. Not at all. Instead, use people's names professionally, with permission, and make a relevant point when doing so. That's how you build credibility and rapport. Have a list of names and stories attached to them that are relevant to the benefits and value of your product or service. It's the names and stories that draw them in.

3. **Uncover their needs**
   You must earn the right to ask to do business with people. You don't show up and say you need this, this, and this and follow that with a request for a check. That won't work, ever. You must take your time and start uncovering their needs and then applying ideal solutions to meet them.
   Remember the E.A.R.N.I.N.G. Sale System in Chapter 3? It will help you stay on track and uncover their needs as you mentally go through

the acronym, Evaluate, Advantages, Revise, No, Interpret, Nothing, Gain. For a free printable version of the E.A.R.N.I.N.G. Sale System, visit www.convertsalesfaster.com.

4. ***Create a buying, not a selling, atmosphere***
This means you are permitting people to say "no." You are letting them off the hook. You might say something like, "If you like it, great. If you don't, it's not a big deal." Watch them relax when you say it. After all, you want them to be at ease and feel like it's okay if they decline your offer. They are expecting a pitch, maybe even expecting a high-pressure pitch, so odds are your no-pressure pitch is new. And they feel this isn't a big deal to you. It reduces any feelings of pressure (a negative emotion that fills the emotional bucket) and makes you look more confident than ever.

5. ***Answer objections***
You have probably heard the saying, "Whoever brings up the objection first wins." It's true. Learn to view objections like tortilla chips: you are on one side of the table, your prospect is on the other, and a pile of chips in the middle. When your prospects hit you with an objection, such as, "I've got a guy already," you have an answer and eat that chip. "I need to check with my spouse," or "I don't have any money," or "I don't have enough time"—it doesn't matter the objection—you are ready to eat their objections.

Bring it up first, eat that chip, increasing your

chances of success. When you bring it up, you take it off the table.

Anticipate and answer their objections in advance, and you clear the table. You know objections don't go away on their own, so face them head-on so you can move past them.

## SKIP THE BRAGGING PART

During the foundation portion of a sale, prospects often ask you, "So, what do you do?"

This happens constantly, and if you follow that lead, it will be a distraction. You are showing up and throwing up if you go down that road. The odds are you will go logical because you are trained that way. To counter that, you need a well-prepared answer that goes something like this:

> *"I work with a handful of people in your organization, helping them with _____ and _____. But if it's all right with you, I'd like to skip the part where I brag about myself and how good and great and wonderful I am. We can pick that up later. I'd like to ask you a couple of questions."*

They always say, "Go ahead." Let's pause here as this is big. I love saying it. Every one of my clients heard me say that on our first call. One sentence that can really set you apart.

From their perspective, they expect you to do the "show up, throw up" pitch where you brag about how good, and great, and wonderful you are, so be different than every other salesperson.

They will never ask you to go back and brag about yourself. It's not needed. And again, this simple step screams confidence.

Subconsciously, they are thinking, "Yes. I don't have to listen to you brag about yourself."

Remember that bragging about yourself doesn't help you at all, anyway.

## ASK DIG-IN QUESTIONS SO THEY FILL THEIR OWN EMOTIONAL BUCKETS

We have previously discussed the two buckets that need to be filled for a sale: the logical bucket and the emotional bucket.

Your voice makes the logical bucket (logical sale), while the emotional bucket (the emotional sale) is made with their voice.

You want your prospects to get emotionally engaged with your offer. When they think hard about it, they will begin to talk about all their concerns and questions, and their emotional bucket will fill up with their own voice. How?

Remember back in Chapter 3, where we talked about dig-in questions? You must get your prospect talking so they look beyond the *what* to define the *why*. If they tell you *what* they want, you *dig* deeper to find out *why* they want it. When it's time to sell, sell that.

To recap, you can't just come right out and ask, "Why do you want that?" That would be a little creepy and will probably ruin your sales presentation.

The answer is getting the same information but coming at it differently. Find your prospect's *why* by using simple dig-in questions:

- What do you mean?
- How so? Tell me more.
- What does that look like?

- Can you give me an example?

- Just for clarity, can you say that again?

- What would that mean for you?

- How will that make your life easier?

- What else?

When you ask these questions, the prospect's own voice is answering. *Their voice is filling up their emotional bucket.*

And the more dig-in questions you ask, the more their emotional bucket will fill up. When that happens, it enables you to really tailor your presentation. They have told you *what* they want and *why.*

For example, let's say you are a financial advisor and the people across the table have just told you, "We want to be comfortable when we retire."

You could respond with, "Great. When you say 'comfortable,' what do you mean by that?"

That's a dig-in question as are these:

> *"What does that look like for you?*
> *Tell me more about that."*
> *"Can you give me an example of that?"*

As they answer your questions, filling up their emotional bucket at the same time, write down their answers. You will need what they say when you close, whether it's in five minutes, five weeks, or five months. Write down what they are saying as it is filling their emotional bucket.

## DIG-IN TO YOUR OWN SELLING

If your prospects are talking, filling their emotional bucket, and selling themselves, while you are asking "dig-in" questions, you can be confident when you close. It's not a risky deal because they are telling you everything you need to close confidently.

Now, consider the sales process from this perspective: the prospect knows you are trying to sell them. They may be willing to hear you out, but they are already mentally listing why they won't buy from you. In a very real sense, they are building a wall of objections between themselves and your product or service. Whenever we build things, we are proud of them, and they are proud of their wall. Good salespeople make sales, meaning they can go over, around, under, or through just about any wall. That is what good salespeople do.

But great salespeople do something different. They help their prospects tear down their own walls.

Now, tearing down walls is hard work, so having your prospects do it is easier. And when you let them tear down their own wall of objections, they are buying—and you aren't even selling.

Until you address the reasons and objections, the wall is still there. Create the right environment with your prospects. You might make a sale, but your new clients may have buyer's remorse. They may think, "Dang it, Joe sold me again."

This very process is how you gain trust, which is the first step toward a true partnership.

When you *earn* the prospect's business and build relationships by asking dig-in questions, you and your prospect remove bricks from that wall. They are lowering their prospects' defenses and negating their objections. This happens every time you get them to fill their emotional bucket.

For a free printable version of the E.A.R.N.I.N.G. Sale System, visit www.convertsalesfaster.com.

### DIG-IN TO YOUR OWN SELLING

A good salesperson might go over, under, around, or through that wall and make a sale, but a great salesperson has them tear down their wall.

## FILLING THEIR EMOTIONAL BUCKET

We have already talked about letting your prospects talk to fill up their own emotional bucket, and most experienced salespeople understand that prospects believe about 25 percent of what you (the salesperson) say. But consider this; your prospect believes 100 percent of what they say.

Of course, they believe their own words, so you need to let them fill up their own bucket. The first time you meet, they fill up their bucket by answering your questions.

If you take your time in that first meeting and write copious notes, you will learn all the important answers to *what* they want and *why* they want it.

Then the next time you meet with them, and their emotional bucket is empty (because it has holes and drains out), you already have what it takes to help them fill it back up again.

You have them say again what they *want* and *why* they want it.

You remind them of what they told you the last time you talked. You might say:

> "I want to clarify one thing you said you were concerned about last time we talked. Can you tell me more about that?"

Whatever it is you are selling, jump back into the conversation stream you had going last time. Let them fill up their emotional bucket again.

You need them to say it. If you repeat what they said when they last filled their bucket, it has little value. If you get them to say it again, it allows their voice to fill their emotional bucket.

It won't take long. Do something like that every time you talk to see where they are emotionally.

For every deal or proposal in your pipeline that has stalled and not yet been sold, this will help to get it moving again.

Think about that for a minute. If you can move your stalled deals forward, whether you get a "yes" or "no," isn't that worth a lot?

A "maybe" is half sold. Your prospect's logical bucket may be full, but their emotional bucket has drained out. Use this opportunity to reengage to fill up their emotional bucket.

If you call in follow-up, leave a voice message that sounds something like this:

"I remember we had a good meeting a while back, and I am looking at some good ideas about what you want. I want to learn more about why you want it, so let's set up a time to talk about it."

Every time you get back in to see them and get them talking about their emotional reasons to buy it is helping refill their emotional bucket.

You may have proposals out there that are three, six, or even twelve months old. Simply waiting does nobody any good. Connect again to get them to refill their emotional bucket.

Either way, the interaction will move you closer to a "yes" or "no." That's what you want because the "maybes" kill you.

And when you are talking with your prospects, take notes. They like it that you keep track of things. It conveys knowledge, respect, organization, trustworthiness, success, and confidence— and that helps them buy.

## HANDLING QUESTIONS MIDSTRIDE

Everyone in sales has been taught to answer questions with other questions. Though that can be effective, it can also be very annoying. We see it all the time and often do it ourselves because we have been trained to do it.

But sometimes, the questions must be answered. Imagine you are midstride, right in the middle of your introduction, and your prospect asks you a question. See if you can turn it into an opportunity to fill their emotional bucket.

For example, suppose your prospect asks, "Can your product do X?" or "Can your service do Y?"

Most salespeople would answer, "Oh, yeah, it's what we do. We do it all the time. In fact, we did it just yesterday. It's what we specialize in." Most salespeople go logical because they are trained to go logical.

It's tempting to answer those very real questions with lots and lots of examples but resist that urge.

Instead, say something like, "We've done it before, but let me ask you a question. I want to make sure I answer your question in the right context. Why is that important to you?"

In other words, when I am asked a question, I think, "Something in her past has caused her to ask that question. I want to know what that is before I answer it. My answers are

100 percent more valuable and tuned to what they want and why they want it.

Then be quiet and wait for the answer. Your prospects give you emotional reasons why your product or service will solve their problems. In so doing, they are filling up their emotional bucket. Then ask some dig-in questions.

What else?

Can you tell me more about that?

What your prospects ask is important, but *why* they asked is even more important. Let me say that again.

*What your prospects ask is important, but why they asked is even more important.*

But most salespeople blow by that important information. They are so busy explaining how they are experts in those areas that they miss the opportunity to have their prospects fill their emotional buckets.

Remember, whoever is talking is buying. If you are talking, then you are buying their objections. But if you get them talking, they are buying whatever you are selling.

So, get them talking. Don't talk yourself out of the sale.

## LEAD YOUR PROSPECTS TO SOLUTIONS

This next section is effective but not something I personally use often. If you follow the emotional sale approach, I find this unnecessary. But as another tool for you, there is the C.H.I.P. Method.

Nobody likes pain or negative emotions. We avoid those things as much as possible. Instead, we gravitate toward positive situations.

Interestingly, we flee the bad faster than we run toward the good. For example, you touch something hot and jerk your hand back quickly. But you don't grab a bowl of ice cream (unless you are one of my daughters) quite so quickly.

## DIG-IN TO YOUR OWN SELLING

Understand that humans are more likely to move away from a negative situation than we are to move toward a positive situation. So, lead your prospects away from negative situations in their lives and toward your better solution.

We all tend to move away from a negative faster than we will move toward a positive. For that reason, it makes sense to sell accordingly, and that means selling to their pain.

The following acronym, C.H.I.P. will help you do exactly that:

*C: Cut.* The prospect brings up an issue. This is their cut.

*H: Hurt.* You need to make it hurt. Make it uncomfortable and awkward for them.

*I: Intensify.* Let them wallow in their pain. It needs to be intense so they really feel it. To intensify is to take the hurt to a deeper level, which is what is necessary to make them act.

*P: Present.* This is where you present a different offer. There is no pain. Your answer is wanted and valuable, and it fills up their emotional bucket.

Applying the C.H.I.P. Method to a sale might look something like this:

Suppose again that you are a financial advisor, and the "C" (cut) is an issue the prospect has with her current advisor. "He only calls me once a year," she laments.

Now you know what the "H" (hurt) is, so you "I" (intensify) it by saying something like, "I'm simply curious. Do you call him once a year, and the call lasts for fifteen to twenty minutes? Or you can go to see him in his office?"

The prospect will say, "Yep, exactly."

To further intensify the hurt, you might ask, "Have you ever thought about questions you needed to ask your financial advisor throughout the year, but when you get to his office, you can't remember them? And you feel awkward and embarrassed because you know you should be asking questions but can't remember them?"

The prospect is thinking, "This person gets it."

You can keep going, intensifying the pain even more, by saying, "What about your quarterly statement? If you're like a lot of people, you look at every number on that statement the first time you get it. The next quarter, you look at most of the numbers. The following quarter, you look at just the bottom two numbers. Before long, you're not even opening that statement anymore. And when your financial advisor talks to you about it, you don't really know what he's saying, so you feel like you're out of the loop."

Now you can sit back and let her wallow in the reality of her current situation. Wait for her to answer. Let her bake a little bit. You want her to sweat it out.

You are not attacking the other person. Rather, you are creating a stark contrast between what she has now and what she could have with you.

You might say something like, "This is what we do. We're going to ensure all your questions are answered throughout the year, and you will always feel in the loop."

Add in or repeat a few answers from your dig-in questions, and you get emotional engagement.

Then you explain how you are different from the competition, which is the opposite of the negative emotions and situation she has faced. She wants to leave the pain but has no idea where to go. And you have the solution.

She sold herself. You listened, applied the C.H.I.P. Method, and she was ready.

## CREATE A COMFORTABLE ENVIRONMENT

You need a comfortable environment to ask dig-in questions that lead to emotional sales. Without the right environment, it may feel weird and awkward. That means you must work to create that comfortable environment from the first moment you meet someone.

As you well know, you can't just start asking dig-in questions. You need to create a space for that.

To set up that space, you (assuming for this example that you are still a financial advisor) could say to your prospect:

I work with my clients differently than you might be accustomed to. I know many advisors spend a lot of time figuring out what you want, crystallizing your goals, and asking what retirement looks like for you. That's important, and we will do that as well, but I want to do something else along with that.

Periodically, I'm going to be asking a lot of *why* questions. Why do you want this, and why do you want that? Sometimes, when I do that, the *why* questions might seem silly. You might not even have an answer right now, and that's fine. Those are all parts of it. But I need to take the time to figure out *what* you want and *why* you want it. Knowing that makes a difference in the type of work I will do for you.

In addition, you need to hear yourself say what you want and why you want it because it crystallizes your thinking. It confirms it, and it allows for course corrections if needed.

The prospect will say, "Yes, that sounds good."

You set up the space you need; this also applies to all future conversations.

In essence, you asked for their permission to make the emotional sale, and they gave it to you.

### DIG-IN TO YOUR OWN SELLING

Get your prospects' permission to make an emotional sale.

# PART IV

# WHAT TO DO AFTER THE SALE STARTS

# 8

# Step 4: Pitch

I f you have done your job on the other parts of the sales cycle, you can now present to your prospects *your* solutions to *their* problems and *their* reasons why they need to buy right now from you. You should have the sale.

They have already told you *what* they want and *why* they want it. If you sell that and only that, they are happy.

You can always add to what they bought, but the key factor is that they bought what they wanted and said why they needed it.

## YOUR PITCH

You are the specialist in what your company offers, whether it's a product or service.

This is what every company's marketing department is all about. They do their job well by providing you with the necessary information, details, and specs from which you create your sales presentation.

Most of their information is the logical part of the sale. It's necessary, and it's what fills the logical bucket. It is also what you talk about. It's your voice talking, filling up that bucket.

Your marketing department has scripted what its product does, how it works, what the benefits are, and more.

Many of you have heard of the "feature-benefit" sales approach. It can be kind of cheesy, but it has a good intent although may not be delivered in the same way.

I would change that approach to where the pitch blends the logical and emotional buckets, resulting in making your product or service needed and wanted.

Most likely, your initial sales training included a script or list you were told to memorize. And then, you were told to give your pitch and watch your prospects as they follow along with the steps of your script.

Isn't that where most people in sales start? But where does most selling take place?

Selling takes place when you have moved above the buying line. The sale takes place there, where you discover their *what* and *why* and where they connect with you at an emotional level.

Your pitch only shows them what they want and repeats why they want it.

If there is a match between what you do in your pitch with what they said they wanted and why they wanted it, then you've got a sale. It's that simple. This assumes you have successfully made both an emotional and a logical sale.

The trick of the pitch is to tailor it to what they say and keep it to what they want or why they want it.

It's about your taking a genuine interest in them. That is how and why prospects grow to like you in return. Remember from before, doctors cannot fix you unless you tell them how or why; you cannot sell anyone unless they tell you how or why.

## YOUR PITCH—SHORT AND SWEET

Take out your pitch, pull out the logical part of the sale, and break it down into bite-size pieces. Then you can pick and choose what's needed.

You don't need to show off. You may have twenty different features and benefits you want to discuss regarding your product or service, but if you are talking to someone interested in only two of them—that's all you should bring up. You can always go back and address the other eighteen if needed.

### DIG-IN TO YOUR OWN SELLING

It's easier to sell what they want to buy
than sell what you want to sell.

Yes, there will be a little bit of flying by the seat of your pants as far as what they know, but that is the nature of sales. Once you break it down, you can interject and add to it. You can always come back and add more features, provided you tie in emotion or realign it to their emotional bucket.

Your pitch should be short and sweet. This is not the time to ramble on and on. Instead, it is time to use your pitch to accomplish what you are here to do: make the sale.

The biggest thing to remember with a pitch is that this is the time when you use what's in their emotional bucket to tie to your features or benefits.

The pitch connects your logical bucket to their emotional bucket. It is that simple.

Close as early as you can, and always tie your pitch to what they just told you a few minutes earlier and blend in their *whys* from their emotional bucket.

## SALES AUDIT

It is safe to say that most of us have a plan for how we think the sale will go—what we will say, how to present, and what will happen—and we are usually wrong. It never goes according to plan.

In addition, how in the heck do you plan to establish rapport at the start of the sale? Sales is messy, disorganized, and goofy.

Because of that, I do a fair number of annual sales audits. They are incredibly helpful. I found that when we are training, an incredible amount of selling information is missed. The trainees don't realize the importance of what you say and what you ask during the pitch. Experienced salespeople operate in the world of unconscious competence (they're so good and have been doing it for so long, they don't even realize what they're doing anymore), hence the trainee thinks they're winging it. But whether you are a trainee or an experienced salesperson, I recommend everyone do a sales audit to ensure you're consistently covering the essential steps within the 7-Step Sales Cycle and filling the logical and emotional buckets for each and every sale. It helps identify those pieces, why they're important, and a method to apply them.

Below are a few sample sales audit questions that isolate key pieces within your pitch that need to be addressed:

- How many dig-in questions did I ask?

- When did they get above the buying line?

- Did I close them?

- Did I get them to say what they wanted?

- Did I get them to say why they wanted it?

- Did I get them to say what it would be like if that issue was fixed?

- Did I get them to say what their job would be like if it was fixed?

- How many trial close questions did I ask?

- How much time did I spend asking questions for them to fill their logical bucket?

- How much time did I spend asking questions for them to fill their emotional bucket?

- Who did most of the talking?

- Can I write down what they wanted?

- Can I write down why they want it in their own words?

- Did I sell to their why?

Write down your answers to these questions for the next ten pitches. It will help you see where you are, increase your awareness, and help program you to do the very things you want to do.

Go to www.sellnothing.co and visit my Success Page or scan the QR code below to share your stories and successes.

# Step 5: Answer Objections

THIS IS SALES, and you are supposed to get more "no" than "yes" replies. That's part of it. Objections are part of selling. Therefore, your whole mindset needs to go with this reality. Accept it. Objections are not a big deal. You need to learn to address objections by having prepped answers; you cannot avoid them.

When it comes to objections, what is it that your prospects need? They need more information, along with constant refilling of their emotional bucket.

## OVERCOMING OBJECTIONS

You can move most prospects away from their objections by using emotional selling. It is the key to anticipating and answering objections.

When I get an objection, my first instinct is to look at the emotional bucket; are they engaged? Did their voice fill it up?

To start, you must know that there are basically three reasons why prospects don't buy from you:

1. They don't know you enough to like you so far.

2. They have not bought into your product or services yet.

3. They don't think what you offer can help them or is not worth the investment.

All objections will fall under one of these categories, therefore you can prepare and address them before they arise.

If you can do that, you are more likely to get the sale. That is precisely why you must address objections upfront before you get into the pitch for your product or service.

Regardless of the objection, more information and more emotion are needed. Without it, people remain confused or unconvinced.

Remember that the objection process is a dialogue, not a monologue. You must engage them and have a conversation. Answering objections is selling, hence you need them talking. Remember, whoever is talking is buying.

Some salespeople who encounter an objection will get all tense and just start firing a lot of questions, bragging about how good and great, and wonderful they are. They go logical and try to refill the logical bucket. That's not going to work. That bucket is still full, and that's not a dialogue.

Again, objections are simply part of selling. Don't freak out. Instead, find answers. You need them, but so do your prospects.

Watch how much they talk, and then ask dig-in questions on top of that.

In truth, you know from experience what type of objections you will receive and when you will receive them. So, it's not much of a surprise, is it?

You want to get them talking when you are answering their objections. You do that by asking dig-in questions, followed by dig-in questions, followed by more dig-in questions.

Never, ever forget that *whoever is talking is buying.* Yes, you need to answer their objections, but you cannot do all the talking, doing the whole monologue thing. No, because you will not close the sale.

## THE FOUR DIFFERENT TYPES OF OBJECTIONS

Objections are not only natural, but they are also good and helpful for your prospects. You are there to add value, and handling objections is a great place to do just that.

Very seldom is an objection an outright "no" to your offer. Usually, they are saying, "I'm not ready yet." They are still in the game, like a fish on a line, and you need to reel them in by providing enough value that they will "yes" themselves into the sale.

### DIG-IN TO YOUR OWN SELLING

Ask yourself, "Am I giving my prospects so much value that they can't help but say 'yes' to my offer?" Give your prospects more value—and you'll get more sales.

Objections fall into four distinct categories:

1. Dollars

2. Decider

3. Delays

4. Desire

- **Dollars.** They simply can't afford it or, more likely, think, "I have money, but I don't have money for this."

- **Decider.** The prospects say, "I need to talk to my spouse" or "I need to talk to the boss." They are trying to have someone else make the decision for them.

- **Delays.** The prospects say, "I'm good with what I have," or "I need to think about it. I don't need to change." They are stuck and see no reason to spend the effort to get up and move on. They may ask, "Can you mail me more information? I need to think about it when I have the time."

- **Desire.** This is where the emotional bucket lives. Their desires equal what they want to fix and why they want it fixed. You can't sell it if they haven't said their why.

You need to identify what type of objection you are dealing with right away. If you can figure it out quickly, it will help you avoid objections, speed the process along, and make more sales.

## THE FORMULA FOR HANDLING OBJECTIONS

Any formula in selling, whether it's an acronym or numbers, is there to help you in the selling process. You know from experience that it is rare to go through all the points in the proper order, so take the best of the ideas below and leave the rest. These steps are listed here in the ideal order, but apply them as you can per interaction.

You will overcome objections when you apply this seven-step formula:

*Step 1: Hear them out.* You must be crystal clear about what the objection is. Listen.

*Step 2: Repeat it back.* Tell them, "I want to make sure I'm hearing you correctly," and then repeat their objection back to them. Now you know you are all on the same page. One of the most frustrating things in sales is going through the process only to find out you haven't addressed their real objection.

*Step 3: Box them in.* You need to make sure you are answering their true objection. Often, the first objection is not the true objection. If you don't clarify, you will be racing from one objection to the next. The answer is to box them in with their objections.

For example, let's say the price is the objection, as it often is. To box them in, say something like, "Other than the financing or the price, is there anything else that's holding you back from going forward?" Let them reply, then offer, "If we had a way to work around the price, would we be ready to move forward?" Now you have just that one objection to deal with.

**Step 4: Transition.** Acknowledge what they said, even if you disagree with it. These transition statements are for you and don't matter. They're for you to make sure you remain focused and not passive. They'll act as your springboard into the next selling step.

**Step 5: Make the resell.** Because whoever is talking is buying, you need to get them talking. Ask something like, "Just curious, what appealed to you about this in the first place?" or "Just curious, why did you take the meeting?" And be quiet. Ask dig-in questions next. This is where you find *what* they want and *why* they want it.

*"What do you mean?"*

*"How so?"*

*"What does that look like?"*

*"Tell me more about that."*

Don't move forward with anything else until you know their *what* and *why*. Better said, don't move forward until you get them to say what they want and why they want it. You are filling or refilling their emotional bucket, no selling, no solutions, no nothing until they are emotionally engaged.

Remember, do not try to sell or resell until they are emotionally engaged.

For example, let's say you are making a husband-and-wife presentation. When you are talking to the wife, asking dig-in questions, the husband hears what she wants and why. She is selling him for you. When you ask the husband some dig-in questions, she listens to *what* he wants and *why*. He is selling her. They are filling up their own emotional buckets, so let them do it. Do not move forward until their emotional buckets are full. And the logic bucket? It's still there, and odds are it's full as well.

Later, when they are on their way home and talking between themselves, they will not be excited about the math in the logic bucket. No, they are going to be talking about *what* they wanted and *why* they wanted it, the very things they told you earlier as they filled their emotional buckets. They are still selling each other, and you are hopefully in a new conversation with your next appointment.

***Step 6: Weak, strongest, stronger.*** Look at it this way: when someone objects, you are in a weak spot. You need to relate the situation to something they have experienced, something they believe, agree with 100 percent, or have dealt with personally in the past. Get to something where they are strongest. We then need to pull things from their strongest to make our weak position stronger. You want to take their strength and bring it forward to where you are now. This gets them emotionally engaged. Take their experience and relate it to where you are and use that same experience as the reason to go forward. For example, when we get an objection, we are in a weak spot. When most salespeople get an objection, they try to give more facts and reasons why their product will work and what it does.

They go to logical selling. This is not the time to sell logically. When we get an objection, we must engage the prospect emotionally.

Here's an example of what it looks like:

Let's say I am a financial advisor talking with long-term clients about making some insurance changes. They both work in the medical field. The objection is that they are good with what they have, the insurance I sold them years ago is good enough, and they don't have the money to make any changes. So, I am weak here. I go to where they are strongest—their work, what they do for a living.

I would say, "Can I ask you a question? You two are both in the medical field, and is it true that it is changing at a rapid pace, where things, procedures, even medications you did three years ago are now considered barbaric? They are constantly coming up with better treatments. I bet there have been times when you wrote a prescription that at the time was the best there was, and now five years later, there is this new prescription that is better and has fewer side effects. Your job as a doctor is to make your patients aware of newer and better treatments. If you don't, are you really serving them? Actually, I bet your patients would be upset if they found out that there was a better treatment, and you didn't tell them. Does that make sense? Give me some feedback on that."

*Tell me more.*

*What else?*

*How so?*

"Well, that's kind of what we are dealing with here. Five years ago, when you bought that insurance, it was the best we had. Now we have some new products, and your situation has also changed. Would it be OK for me to just educate you on what has changed? Before I do, I am just curious as to the reasons for having insurance in the first place. Have those also changed?"

*Can you give me an example?*

*What would that look like?*

*Tell me more.*

Notice the dig-in questions and the emotional filling of the bucket. Remember, it's their voice, not mine, that fills it.

Now I can go fill the logical bucket.

Another quick example. I have good kids, but they are kids, and we're in the process of learning responsibility. It dealt with them doing their chores. We had a talk and thought we were good. A few days later, they asked if they could bike to the lake to go swimming. I asked, "Are your chores done? If so, you can go." After they went, I found out that the chores were not done. So, I called them and said they needed to fix it ASAP. I expected them to come home—they did two hours later. I was a bit upset, so I asked them why they didn't come home right away like I had asked. They said they had invited some friends to the lake too and didn't think it was right to leave them.

I was in a weak spot; I went to where they were strongest. Tell me more about that:

I heard it would be rude just to leave them. They shouldn't treat friends that way. It would not be respectful.

Their friends expected them to be there, and following through is important.

I took what they said, where they are strongest and made my weak position stronger, "So, if I am hearing you right, you said that you didn't want to be rude, you need to treat your friends the right way, you want to be respectful, and you want to make sure your friends can count on you."

"Yes, Dad."

"Well, shouldn't those same things apply to Mom and me?"

This got them. They couldn't argue against their own words, which were pivotal in changing their thinking.

Here's a third example of Weak, Strongest, Stronger dealing with price—the most common objection.

Let's say you are selling to Sally, an insurance agent interested in hiring you as a coach for her agency. She is interested and asks relatively early in the pitch, "So, how much is this going to cost?" This is my weak point, as I am not ready to give the cost as I have not had her fill her emotional bucket yet. If she asks for a price now and I give her a number, I might as well go bang my head against the wall.

You could reply, "I'm curious, Sally, when you talk to a new potential client, you recognize the importance of first impressions and professionalism. You don't want to have to backtrack or clarify something right out of the gates, right? There are a lot of things you need to know before you can give them a quote. Once you have all the required info, you must still price-shop it with the carriers.

You really can't give them an accurate price upfront. In fact, it could even work against you if you gave them a ballpark number to start with and the actual number is much larger. It is better to wait until you can give them an accurate number. I want to do the same here; once I understand what you want and need, we can discuss price. Does that sound good?"

They need to hear you out before you can answer their "what's it going to cost?" question. They need to get all the details. And they need to fill up their emotional bucket. Then you go right back into it: Let them talk. Whatever they say, they are selling themselves for you. You don't even need to sell anymore.

Another reason some prospects jump right to the "how much is it" question is because their emotional bucket is not yet full. Fill up that emotional bucket, and the price question usually happens at the proper time. Follow that with some dig-in questions, and let them keep on selling themselves. Prospects are much more receptive to thinking up the ideas than you telling them the ideas.

Always remember that prospects who give you objections most likely have an empty emotional bucket. Return to a point of strength, such as why they set up a meeting with you. "Hey, just curious," I'll say, "you have a lot of things on your calendar. Why did you set time out to talk to me?" Let them talk, then ask some more dig-in questions like:

*"What else?*

*Tell me more about that.*

*What does that look like?"*

Dig in, and let them fill their emotional bucket. That will keep you on track more than anything else. Use dig-in questions to let them fill their emotional bucket. Then, get them to the logical answer to their objections.

## DIG-IN TO YOUR OWN SELLING

Another reason some prospects jump right to the "how much is it" question is because their emotional bucket is not yet full. Fill up that emotional bucket, and the price question usually happens at the proper time.

*Step 7: Reclose.* It's time to close but close the second time in a slightly different way than you closed the first time. If you use the same words, they will think, "Wait, I've heard this before, and I already said 'no,' so why are we here again?" Always use different words on the second or third close.

# PART V

# WHEN TO FINISH AND START THE NEXT SALE

# 10

# Step 6: Close

I F YOUR PROSPECTS are emotionally bought in, you really don't need to close.

Did you hear that?

Most salespeople have been taught that the sale happens at the close. Or that the most important part of the selling process is the close.

The close is part of the overall selling cycle. It's a single step of many. So don't put all the pressure on yourself to make the sale at the close.

If you get all worked up, building pressure, and hyper-focusing on the close, your prospects will sense it. You are telegraphing, "Hey, this is a big deal." They're going to get worked up as well.

The close is just a natural part of the sale; it does not need to become a big deal. They know it, you know it, so don't freak out.

Treat it as simply a step in the process, and that takes pressure off everyone.

Now, that does not mean the close is not important. Not at all. The close is needed, but it's not the finish line, so relax.

## PREPARATION FOR THE CLOSE

The best way to prepare for the close is to walk your prospects through all the previous steps in the 7-Step Selling Cycle.

Everything leads up to this point, the next step in the process. The logical next step is the close.

### DIG-IN TO YOUR OWN SELLING

It is easier to sell prospects what they want to buy, once they have told you what they want and why they want it.

If your prospects say, "Where do I sign up?" or "What's next?" you know they have emotionally sold themselves. They are ready. They want to act because their emotional bucket is full.

The close is simply a crystallization of what should happen next. They are sold logically and emotionally.

You both know *what* they want and *why* they want it. You provided a solution to the challenges they faced and now you allow them to buy it.

It's pretty easy, really. They are buying what they want, not what you are trying to sell them.

I may be oversimplifying this, but the close to me is simply talking through the logistics of what comes next.

## CONFIDENCE REQUIRED

In your close, confidence is vital. There can be no wiggle room here. Confidence is an absolute requirement.

If you have gone through the entire 7-Step Selling Cycle using dig-in questions, you know every *what* and *why*, the emotional and logic buckets are full, and you will be confident. How could you not be?

One extra piece of confidence is a close that is memorized.

You do not have time at this point in the sales process to have your brain going on tangents or even thinking about what you will say. It simply needs to come out of your mouth the exact same way, word for word, each time.

If the thought of a word-for-word close scares you or you dismiss it because it feels "robotic," it may be best to start looking for another job. Here's why. Think of how hard you worked to get that referral, that name, to make that call, set up that appointment, have multiple sales calls, and all the effort you put into getting to this point—only an idiot would allow themselves to be passive enough to be robotic at such a critical part in the sale.

Here is another reason scripts are important. Most people in a sales situation are thinking, "What should I say next?" They're not listening. Having a memorized script, you know what you're going to say and can listen at another level.

So, get good at your close—memorize your close and make it your own. A trick that I do is insert a forced chuckle or laugh into it. The forced laugh forces you to be present. The close is not the place to be passive or weak.

I often use phrases like, "Is it okay if I ask a question?" or "Can I ask a question?" in the beginning parts of the sale, but I do not use those words at all during the close.

Why? Because those phrases are useful when selling to soften things and generate responses. They are also non-threatening and more passive in nature.

But when you are closing, it is not the time to be passive at all. It is time for confidence. The close is assumptive in nature, and that is confidence on display. This can be taken too far, so be careful with assuming things, but most people should be more assumptive with their close.

The close demands confidence, so practice until the close is natural, word for word.

You are intentional, and yet you are there to serve. After all, you have helped them overcome obstacles, clarify what is most important, and find answers to their problems. All the hard work has been done and done well.

Lastly, avoid all distractions. Distractions in the close shift the focus away from your prospects, which can be fatal. For example, you're in the closing step and it's going well, then you remember another key feature. Naturally, you want to bring it up thinking it will confirm the sale. I recommend not bringing it up at this time. Continue to close. You need to stay 100 percent focused. If you get an objection, bring up the key feature when you're reselling.

If it does not distract and the close is successful, bring it up to add more value and solidify the sale. Distractions make you look less confident and talk past the close (see the buying curve below).

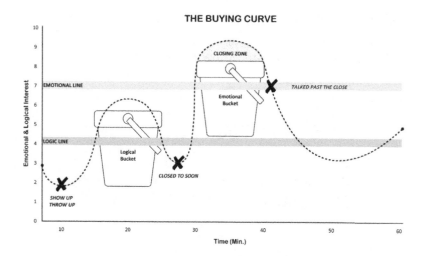

## CLOSING EARLY

Close early. The fact is most salespeople don't close early enough.

With all the details of closing, there is one that holds true, no matter how well you might have memorized your closing script: *If you close too late, you'll miss the sale.*

Instead, look for ways to close earlier and earlier in your sales presentation, of course when you are above the buying line.

## ASSUME THE SALE

Your close must also be an assumptive close. It really goes without saying that you are assuming the sale. After all, you have done all the work to get here.

What's more, it is impossible not to be assumptive when you have their emotional bucket full. You just solved their problems, so why would you not assume the sale?

You could back up if you need to by saying, "I'm sorry, I

thought you wanted this, and based on what you said, I was moving forward."

If that happens, simply return to their objection, address it, and then close again.

## DIG-IN TO YOUR OWN SELLING

If you're selling to a prospect that has told you that your product/service answers their needs, how could you not be confident in closing?

A "no" at this point is pretty much a sign of one of two things:

1. They have not filled their emotional bucket enough, or

2. You have not filled their logical bucket.

Of these two options, almost always, it is the emotional bucket that is not full.

Whose job is it to fill these buckets? It's your job.

Yes, they fill their own emotional bucket, but you lead them to do it. And if the logical bucket is empty, that's your job entirely.

When all is said and done, your job is to make sure their emotional and logical buckets are full. After that, you can pretty much assume the sale.

What if their emotional bucket is not full? Odds are, you will hear, "I need to think about it. Call me next month." So what should you do?

In most, if not all cases, the answer is to go back and have them fill their emotional bucket. Then they are ready for the close.

## USE TRIAL CLOSES

Trial closes, except for the close, can be used anytime during the sale cycle. Often, I'm asked when a trial close can be used. My answer—at hello.

A trial close is like taking your prospect's temperature. You ask questions to gauge their interest. It lets you know when they are done and ready for the close. Some examples of trial closes are:

- Does that make sense?

- Do you follow me?

- Just curious, what are you thinking?

- Give me some feedback on what you are hearing?

- Ya with me?

If you use enough trial closes throughout the 7-Step Selling Cycle, you should know when to close and get a "yes."

You should not be surprised. In fact, you should get to a point where you are surprised if you get a "no." It does happen, but not regularly.

If they are logically and emotionally sold, one close is usually all that's needed. However, if an extra close is needed due to an objection or not having filled their emotional bucket, then do it.

## 11

# Step 7: Ask For Referrals

When we started selling, we sucked at everything. We were horrible. Every piece of the sale was a struggle. But through time and repetition, we got pretty good. Most of my clients have gotten to the point where they are between an eight to ten on a scale of one to ten. It could be from countless attempts and much repetition, but they've become experts at certain steps, such as creating trust, answering objections, or making the emotional sale. But I have found that those same people on the eight to ten scale are still rookies when it comes to asking for referrals. Exponential growth happens when this piece of their business reaches the same level in scale.

It's our thinking that needs to change first. When I'm coaching, I ask my clients about their demeanor when selling to a "qualified prospect." The most common answers are:

- Positive
- Upbeat

- Confident

- Engaged

- Relaxed

- Focused

- Energetic

- Confident

Then I ask, do you have a good picture of what that person is like? That is the person that needs to ask for referrals.

In sales, we can be the positive, upbeat, and confident person when we are selling, but when it comes to asking for referrals, we downshift and act passive like a rookie. The ask feels something like, "I kinda, sorta, maybe would like to potentially ask for a referral. Oh, never mind. Here's my business card."

Now that is an exaggeration, but it is a common mindset. Most people are passive when asking for referrals. In my mind, there is nothing passive about asking. *Referrals are more important than the sale.* Here are two examples:

> ***From One to Eighty:*** When I sold for Tom James, I made a presentation to an advisor at Lutheran Brotherhood (now Thrivent Financial). He was not interested in buying a custom suit, but I still asked him for referrals. He gave me four names of people who might be interested because he saw something in me that reminded him of what he was like at my age and wanted to help. The referral tree that started with a "no" grew to over eighty clients at that one company. Without those referrals, there is no way I could have acquired all that business.

***From One to 150:*** The same thing happened when I met with a top executive at the St. Paul Companies, Inc. (now Travelers Insurance). I made one sale, asked for referrals, and received three names. Two years later, I had 150 clients there, not to mention my own parking space and ID pass.

Tell me again how important referrals are. Referrals are a really big deal. They should never be left to chance, glossed over, "winged" (as many say), or forgotten entirely.

## DIG-IN TO YOUR OWN SELLING

There is nothing passive about referrals.

I strive to practice what I preach. Sell Nothing, LLC was founded in 2017. Until recently (2023), I did not have a website and was a ghost on the world wide web. My social media use was extremely limited, with only a LinkedIn profile I never used. I rarely did seminars and never spoke on podcasts or other media outlets. I practiced what I preached. My business was 100 percent based on referrals, growing into what it is today.

## DIG-IN TO YOUR OWN SELLING

Asking for referrals is simply a part of the selling process—nothing more and nothing less. So, get good at it.

## AFRAID TO ASK FOR REFERRALS?

During years and years of coaching, I have asked hundreds of salespeople to role-play their referral ask. I saw that they were most commonly passive, "winging it," and not prepared. Asking for the referral was an afterthought; more importantly, there was zero confidence.

The positive, upbeat, confident person presented earlier disappeared. What was left was someone who sounded like a rookie.

A large percentage of professional salespeople out there don't ask for referrals, much less don't set weekly referral goals. They're not even trying.

### DIG-IN TO YOUR OWN SELLING

Referrals are given to confident people.

Here's an example of how I would coach one of my clients. I would ask:

- Are you good at what you do?
- Are you one of the best in the city?
- Do you have a good product?
- Do you take care of your clients?
- Do you have a good company behind you?

I'll hear yes to all those questions. Then I say:

So, you're good at what you do. You're one of the best in the city. You have a good product. You take care of your clients and have a good company behind you. *If you don't ask* for referrals, someone else, who is not all those things, will be working with your client's friends and relatives. It's kind of like they need us more than we need them.

That simple thought can be a game changer.

The fear, of course, is that a client or prospective client will say, "No, I'm not going to send people I know to you." But that rarely happens. Very rarely. Even if you don't get the sale, your prospects are more inclined to give you referrals than not, especially if they are emotionally engaged.

Magnifying the perceived negative outcome in our minds is called "mental mushrooming." We let negativity's small potential grow until it completely overshadows reality.

The reality is that prospects and clients (people in general) want to help you. When they know what you offer, they can easily connect you with others who also need it. It's really not a big deal at all.

Trust is the foundation of successful selling. It is also the foundation for receiving referrals.

Let's say, for example, you are a realtor. You have established a high level of trust with clients by nurturing the relationship over time. And now these clients trust you enough to sell their homes and help them buy bigger ones.

On a scale of 0 to 100 (100 being the highest), your client's trust in you to sell their home is on the high side. Asking for referrals is a much lower level of trust.

The truth is, getting a referral from your clients requires a lot less trust than it takes to make the sale.

Therefore, it makes no logical sense to fear asking for a referral from an established client. The problem is in your mind. There are different levels of trust.

Let's say I was in town visiting and I am having coffee with a client. I realize that I forgot my billfold in my car and ask if it would be OK for them to buy the coffee and I'll pay them back later—odds are they would. It may be a bit weird or awkward but it's coffee. A low level of trust is needed to buy coffee.

Now let's say I am having coffee with a client, and I ask to borrow $500K and that I will pay them back. Much different reaction here. This is a different level of trust. I think we all get that; now let's apply that to the referral ask.

## DIG-IN TO YOUR OWN SELLING

In The Buying Curve, there is a referral line, similar to the buying line that your prospect needs to cross before you close (see below). You may ask for referrals right away, part way through, or at the end—or all of the above. It's different with each client.

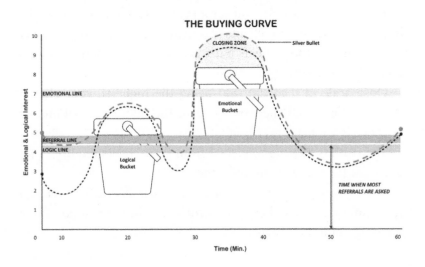

THE BUYING CURVE

It's totally illogical, but that is exactly how most people in sales approach referrals.

If you have established any trust in the selling process, feel free to ask for referrals. You've earned them.

Without a clear plan, asking for a referral will not be smooth and far less effective.

Previously, we discussed the 7-Step Selling Cycle and how to move through the steps. We don't just jump to the close and say, "You need this much term insurance, this much disability, now cut me a check." The same steps need to be applied to referrals. You don't just jump to the close with a referral and ask, "Who do you know?"

## DIG-IN TO YOUR OWN SELLING

Referrals should be treated like a sale.

## ANTICIPATE REFERRAL OBJECTIONS

In sales, we answer objections in advance. The same is true for referrals. There are only two reasons you might not get a referral:

1. You didn't ask.

2. You asked, and they had an objection.

That's it. There are no other reasons. Now, if you didn't ask for referrals, why not? Did you forget or did you not feel comfortable asking for them?

Sometimes it's a combination of both, but most salespeople fail to ask for referrals because they are not comfortable doing so. That is rookie thinking.

If you treat the referral request like it's a sale, you will address objections that might come your way. As you know with selling, whoever brings up the objection first wins. You must do that when you are asking for referrals.

Here are four reasons why your request for referrals might hit an objection:

*Referral Objection 1: Worry that you will embarrass them.* Clients don't want to be embarrassed, ever. Imagine being at a holiday party when your friend comes up and says, "Hey, why in the heck did you give Joe Pallo my name? The guy's been calling me off the hook." Always be professional and tell them that you will treat them the right way.

*Referral Objection 2: Your client does not know or trust you yet.* You can deal with that simply by building your relationship over time and filling their emotional bucket during the selling process.

*Referral Objection 3: Worry that you might hurt their business relationships.* If you are always professional, this should not be a worry. But if you see a client hesitating for this reason, it is important to get it out into the open and discuss it. This is in their head, their thinking. You might learn something valuable that you need to approach differently. Be courageous. Ask, "Why?" and then listen carefully. Emotionally filling their bucket usually fixes this.

*Referral Objection 4: Your client can't think of anyone.* This can be addressed if this is true and not just a delay tactic. It's up to you to solve it.

If you ask for referrals in a planned, professional, confident manner, most, if not all, of the referral objections can be addressed.

## DIG-IN TO YOUR OWN SELLING

Whoever brings up the objection first, wins.

## SCRIPT YOUR REFERRAL REQUEST

Remember, odds are you are still a rookie at asking for referrals, and rookies need scripts. When you were a rookie, you got better with practice and more practice. That is exactly how you get better at asking for referrals.

You already have a way to approach prospecting, setting appointments, conducting first and subsequent meetings, closing the sale, and following up. You may not have it written down formally, but you know it by heart.

The best way to give referrals the priority they deserve is to build them into your plan and work them into your sales presentations.

Does it need to be scripted? Yes, you should start with a script. Follow it at first, but it will soon be a natural part of your selling process.

Write out your script, practice it, and refine it. Video yourself or practice it in front of someone close to you. Ask for feedback. Refine again.

Keep doing this until you feel comfortable with what you are saying. Within no time, it will be smooth and come easily.

Here are seven ideas that you may want to apply to your script.

They are in no particular order, and you can "take the best and leave the rest" approach to what feels comfortable.

1. ***Transition Statement:*** This is purely for you and is simply a statement that tells you that you're about to ask for a referral and to remain positive, upbeat, and confident. Consider it as an "on" switch. As an example, mine is, "Can I ask a favor? I am wondering if you could help me out." It doesn't matter what they are. It is just for you.

2. ***Cell Phone:*** One important thing to me is customer service and good communication. I'll ask, "Is your phone nearby? Can you put my phone number in your cell?" Here's why:

   a. It's warm and fuzzy, good service.

   b. I've passed a mental threshold once my name is in their cell.

   c. I'm removing their objection of not knowing anyone to refer because every name they will think of is already in their phone.

3. ***Share some good news.*** People want to do business with successful people. Warning: Don't take it too far. You don't want to come off as bragging.

4. ***Share a goal, something you're working toward.*** More suited for younger salespeople. Most successful people get to a point where they want to reach down and help someone else up. They see a younger version of themselves in you and want to help.

5. **Have a specific ask that you use word for word.**
   Mine is, "Based on who you know, and the person
   you are, who are three people at your level, in your
   phone, that I should meet?" Then I follow up with,
   "Here's how I will treat them. I'll treat them like
   gold. I just want to connect with them. If they like
   me, great. If not, I'll leave them alone."

6. **Be prepared to have multiple asks or closes for
   referrals.**

7. **Offer Feedback.** "Hey thanks for the referrals. I'll
   make sure that I get back to you and let you know
   which ones hung up on me when I mentioned your
   name." Here's why I say that:

   a. It breaks the ice and inserts a little humor. It's
      also common courtesy.

   b. If they give me three referrals and they all
      go nowhere, I owe that client a callback. It's
      a great message to say, "Hey, thanks for the
      referrals. I connected with the guys, and
      they're all taken care of. I appreciate it." This
      is the right thing to do, but in their mind,
      they'll think of who else they know. I'm
      planting the seed for more referrals.

   c. I owe that client a callback if they give me
      three referrals and all set a meeting. It's a
      great message to say, "Hey, thanks for the
      referrals. I connected with the guys and had
      meetings set with all of them. I appreciate it."
      In their minds, they start thinking of who

else they know. I'm planting the seeds for more referrals.

## SILVER BULLETS

As you may recall, in Chapter 5: Data Gather, I do not count referrals unless a silver bullet is attached. Referrals are worthless without them.

When your clients are giving you names of referrals, don't interrupt. If they say, "You should call Jeff Anderson," simply write down the name. Resist the temptation to ask, "Great. How long have you known Jeff, and how do you know him?"

You have programmed your client's brain to search for names to give you, so let that program run for as long as possible. Any question you ask will shut down the mental search engine. Your only job at this point is to collect the names. Keep them going by saying:

- This is awesome.
- Thanks a lot.
- I appreciate it.
- This helps a ton.
- Is there anybody else?

If they give you additional info, write it down, but don't ask for more info at this time.

When they are done, go back to the first person on the list. Say something like, "Mary Smith, tell me about her," and start gathering data and silver bullets.

# THE TRAITS OF YOUR IDEAL CLIENTS— THE IDEAL REFERRAL DEAL

Some of the best referrals you can get come from your ideal clients and often they have similar character traits. When I ask people, "Who are your ideal clients?" I follow that question by asking what characteristics make them ideal.

Over the years, I have compiled a list of those characteristics or traits. Here are just a few examples of those desirable clients, simply people who:

- Want help.

- Have batteries included (don't drain you of energy).

- Care about their families.

- Are smart, but don't feel the need to prove it. Are more security-minded than gambling-minded.

- Will protect themselves from themselves (recognize and curb their bad habits).

- Are positive and upbeat.

- Are coachable.

- Communicate well.

- Are self-starters.

- Are trusting.

- Are appreciative.

- Are passionate about something.

- Are prompt.

- Have big dreams for the future.

- Think big.

- Plan ahead.

- Are fun.

- Have a sense of humor.

- Are a joy to work with (dealing with them doesn't feel like work).

This is a great list. Wouldn't it make your life easier if all your clients had character traits like that? That would be a great job.

It is possible to do that. Yes, it truly is.

How? Let your clients know these are the character traits you are looking for in their referrals.

So how do you ask for referrals who have these ideal traits?

Begin by writing your list of ideal client character traits. Reduce it to ten to fifteen qualities that are most important to you.

Then, when you meet with a client and get to the point in the meeting where you ask for referrals, you can say, "Hey, can I ask a favor?" When the client says "yes," which they always do, you reply:

> I'm not sharing this with all my clients, just the ones I've gotten to know pretty well—the ones, like you, I've clicked with, the ones I respect, the ones I consider friends. Like it or not, you're on that list. I hope it doesn't come across the wrong way, but I'm having a great year. I'm up about 10 percent in my business.
>
> It's growing, but I'm really focused on building my business with the right people. In other words, I'm looking for a point when, in three to five years, all my clients are my friends—people who think along

similar lines as I do. I've got a list of character traits most of my friends and clients have. You have a lot of these traits. Is it OK to share this list with you? These are some traits of people I like to work with. My ideal clients are people who …

Read the list aloud, then hand it over to your client to read.

When you do this, you will get referred in different circles because you compliment your clients by saying they have ideal character traits. Reading your shortlist out loud is bound to affect them, give them energy, and make them feel good. It will fire you up, and it will fire them up.

Incidentally, this character list helps create an ideal referral-gathering atmosphere.

You emotionally engage them when they read or hear the list, which is a great time to ask for referrals. The emotional bucket is being filled.

When you compliment your clients, it goes a long way to enhance your relationship, making them want to give you more referrals.

## DIG-IN TO YOUR OWN SELLING

It is much easier to ask for referrals by character traits than by job titles.

## MY MOST EFFECTIVE REFERRAL ASK— THE SIMPLIFIED REFERRAL ASK

This is by far my most effective way to get referrals. I have used it for years and it is pure gold. My business is 100 percent referral based, and until now, I have not invested in any marketing. I didn't need to.

Imagine an eight-year-old company in the consulting space, not having a website or any social media pages (until now), not doing a lot of public speaking, not doing any podcasts (until now), and yet growing each year from doing one thing: The Simplified Referral Ask. Here it is:

Imagine there is an empty bucket; this one is labeled "those things." It is filled up with their words, as the "power" is in their voice, not mine.

Before I ask for referrals, I need their voice to fill up that bucket. I won't ask for referrals until it is full. Here is what it sounds like:

"Hey, Nick, we have been working together for eight years and have seen tremendous growth from where you were to where you are. You are number one in FFA mortgages in the US. Your team doubled their production. We have worked on recruiting and staffing issues. You have navigated the referral partnerships to where you are 'the go-to guy.' I just wanted some feedback on what you like about working with me, my team, and the modules. What has worked really well?"

Be quiet. Let him talk; let him fill up that bucket labeled those things.

What else? Tell me more. (Dig-in questions.)

Once the bucket is full of why he liked working with me and what we have accomplished, he is full. I pivot and ask, "Nick, who are three people at your level who would appreciate those things?"

It is that simple.

Whatever words, thoughts, or ideas he put into that bucket are the exact same words, thoughts, or ideas as to why he should refer me to good, qualified people. It works.

## REFERRAL RECAP

This chapter requires a recap because referrals are more important than the sale. Everyone in sales must get better at asking for referrals. Use this referral recap to help keep the details in order:

1. *Understand* why referrals are so incredibly important and treat them as such.

2. *Recognize* that referrals, just as sales, require a foundation of trust with your clients.

3. *Anticipate* objections you might get when asking for referrals, and be prepared to address them confidently.

4. *Realize* you are doing your clients a favor by offering stellar service to their friends and colleagues.

5. *Develop* a script to request referrals and practice it until it's smooth and natural.

6. *Use* visual props to show your clients that you receive many referrals.

7. *Build* a "hot list" or "feed list" of names you collect and manage daily.

8. *Resist* the urge to ask questions about referrals as your clients give the names to you.

9. *Qualify* your referrals to only work with those who match your ideal client's traits.

10. *Request* silver bullets, along with names and phone numbers, for your referrals.

11. *List* the traits of your ideal clients and ask for referrals who have those traits.

# 12

# What Versus Why

THIS CHAPTER WAS the hardest one to write. It's actually where my book stopped initially. It sat here for a year, 90 percent finished, and the wheels fell off. I just could not move forward.

So, this book sat untouched for a year. I am sure it was frustrating for Henry DeVries, my publisher, because I couldn't get it going, yet I wouldn't let it go. I wasn't sure if it was creative avoidance, fear of failure, or not thinking big enough—all things I coach on. He kept at me, and I am glad he did.

Finally, I said, "All right." I took a day, went off, and started coaching myself. Kind of like self-medication, I took myself through my E.A.R.N.I.N.G. Sale System, and I asked a ton of dig-in questions: Why is that? Give me an example.

I made myself ask the questions and write out the answers, and it took about four hours.

And finally, it hit me. It's like, *Pallo, you dork.*

I strive to practice what I preach and take my own medicine. I coach people that "what people want is important, but the real value is why they want it." I took that thought and delivered it here, with this book that offers a lot of what to say and what to do. But the real value is your why, which I will help you find.

This entire book is about the importance of a logical and emotional sale, and both pieces are important. And I think I did a really good job explaining the difference, not to break my arm patting myself on my back.

My thinking was that all I've done is talk about the logical way to make an emotional sale, but I have not talked about the emotional side of selling—about what motivates us. I realized that I should offer the emotional reasons someone will read this and apply the logical pieces. Otherwise, all the ideas, techniques, scripts, and processes may be wasted and not applied if I don't touch on your why. You may not do any of this until your emotional bucket is full.

Looking back on my experiences with coaching and leading teams, I see they are influenced by my former mentor, Jim McEachern, founder of Tom James, a great coach and a super guy. One of the many wise things he asked is, "What do you think is more important than anything?" That question resonated with me. Your thinking is more important than anything. Everything you have read until now is good, but until you are emotionally engaged, it doesn't matter.

I started applying it to my coaching—helping people fill their emotional bucket. When I start working with a client, one of the first things I'll do is simply ask them, "Would you agree with the statement that most people do not know what they want?"

"Yes, I agree with that."

I'll follow up with, "Would you also agree that most people

who know what they want do not write it down?" That's important, too.

"Yes, I'll agree with that."

I'll say, "Okay, so knowing what you want is important. Writing it down is really important. But you know what's extremely important?" And I hear all sorts of answers. It's extremely rare, though, that someone gets to the why.

## DIG-IN TO YOUR OWN SELLING

Knowing what you want is important.
Writing it down is really important.
But what's extremely important, is why you
want it.

If your why is strong enough, what and how don't matter. Think about all the times you've gone through goal setting. I've done it. You've done it.

It's mid-December, and your manager wants your goals for the next year, so you randomly think up a number. It's just a number, so you say you want a 10 percent increase (or whatever you choose). There's nothing there—there's nothing to your choice. Nothing connects your activity (the logical part of your job) to the emotional one.

I am taking my own medicine that I give my clients and am giving it to you. Let's talk about vision.

My first action item with my clients is to help them tell me their why. I have them do something old school by creating a goal notebook or a vision board. Something visual that we look at. Our mind speaks the language of pictures.

As a silly example, you think of a banana if I say *banana*. Our minds' preferred language is pictures; our minds' first language is pictures.

We get what we think about. So, my first action with my clients is to have them create a vision board. It's a piece of cork with a frame around it and has pictures of what they want in different areas of their life: financial, spiritual, educational, emotional, familial, and social. I can't work with one area of my client's life without it bleeding over and touching the others.

Either Jim McEachern or Spencer Hays taught me to ask my clients to do this in terms of "be, do, and have."

The haves are the easy things. They are the consumables and mile markers. But if that's all that motivates you, you may be a bit materialistic. You have to be more than that.

The dos are, "What do you want to do?" such as places you want to go, people you want to meet, and the things you want to do. These are a bit harder to articulate and get nailed down.

The biggest one is, "Who do you want to be?" What type of role model do you want to be to your kids? What type of spouse do you want to be? What type of person will you be in the church and the community? That's the one we want to focus on.

Your vision board should have different elements of be, do, and have. I challenge people to get their family involved, specifically their spouses. They want to get involved. Sometimes they just don't know how, but a vision board gives them a way to participate. It also allows for the "I didn't know you wanted that" ideas to emerge. This is extremely important or useful when those conversations arise that deal with, "When are you coming home again?" If our spouses have a clearer picture, it becomes a "you're doing this for us versus you are doing this for you." Provided your vision board has enough of the "Who do you want to be?" points on it.

If you have young kids, having them think about goals and goal setting is a good idea. I try to talk to my kids about what they want to do. That's the start of their vision boards and their motivation. That's the leverage we have and the why with your kids.

I'm challenging everyone reading this book to create a vision board. It is pictures and may be corny, but we all know it works. The most powerful thing is our goals and why we want them because this fills your emotional bucket.

So, the first piece is being clear about your vision. What you say is important, but your reason why is critically important. Like in selling, I have my clients tell me what they want; then I ask dig-in questions to help them tell me why and sell or coach them to that. In coaching, I have them do the same; the goal of this chapter is to help you do the same.

Be able to say what you want and why you want it.

I have my clients tell me why they want it. I take time out of our coaching calls to let them explain their vision board. Because I need to hear it, but more importantly, they need to hear themselves say it. This is their voice filling their emotional bucket. That's my leverage as a coach to get them to do something different. That's their leverage for themselves to get themselves thinking differently. What they want is important, but why they want it is even more important.

This is my challenge: work on this piece before you go on to the other parts of the book. Your vision is what fills your emotional bucket. Without it, odds are you won't act or think differently, kind of like your clients who are logically sold but not emotionally sold. They won't move forward. Nor will you.

## DIG-IN TO YOUR OWN SELLING

Knowing what you want is important.
Writing it down is really important.
But what's extremely important is why you
want it.

As a last thought and favor, if you have gained something from reading *How To Sell Nothing: The Logical Way To Make The Emotional Sale* or applied an idea that worked, please go to www.sellnothing.co and share it under "Success Stories."

# APPENDIX

# APPENDIX A: KEY TAKEAWAYS FROM EACH CHAPTER

## CHAPTER 1: WHAT'S BEHIND THE CURTAIN

Influence can come from unexpected sources. The influential figures in Joe Pallo's life were not intentionally seeking to have an impact. This reminds us that anyone can profoundly influence others through their actions, teachings, and values, even without awareness.

Whether it's through resilience and faith, leadership through action, positive attitude, and thinking big, ethical decision-making and integrity, or supportive partnership, the key intentions of sharing these stories are:

1. Express gratitude

2. Inspire personal growth

3. Encourage influencing others

Joe hopes that this book and the stories shared will influence you, the reader, in a positive way. He hopes that it encourages you to apply what resonates, aspire to become influential figures in others' lives, and pursue your dreams with determination.

## CHAPTER 2: REMEMBER, WE ALL SELL THE SAME STUFF

The Power of Differentiation in Sales:

1. Stand Out: Differentiation helps you stand out from the competition, making it easier for potential customers to notice and remember you. It creates a unique identity and separates you from the sea of sameness.

2. Avoid Boredom: Being different keeps your sales approach fresh and interesting. Presenting something new and unexpected captures attention and engages potential customers more effectively than repetitive, generic pitches.

3. Offer Unique Value: Differentiation allows you to offer a unique value proposition. By focusing on what sets you apart, you can highlight your product or service's specific benefits and advantages to customers, making it more appealing and compelling.

4. Pitfalls of Selling the Same "Shit": Many salespeople inadvertently fall into the trap of selling the same "shit" as their competitors. Relying on generic sales pitches and minor variations limits their ability to make a lasting impact and win customers over.

5. Authentic Differentiation: To achieve genuine differentiation, break free from the cycle of similarity and establish an authentic and unique selling proposition.

6. Start with Yourself: Your personality, expertise, and ability to connect with customers can set you apart. Authenticity, genuine care, and building strong relationships become invaluable assets.

7. Emphasize Emotion and Relationships: Selling based on emotions and relationships creates a customer connection that transcends product features or price. Building trust, understanding their needs, and offering personalized solutions will make you unbeatable.

8. Focus on Value Delivery: Emphasize your value by showing customers how your product or service solves their problems, improves their lives, or fulfills their desires.

9. Differentiate through Language: Tailor your message to resonate with your target audience, using terms and expressions that align with their needs, preferences, and values.

10. Embrace Change: Challenge the status quo and be willing to evolve. Constantly assess and refine your sales approach to make it more unique and impactful.

Differentiation is not about superficial variations or empty claims. It's about delivering genuine value, building relationships, and presenting a fresh perspective that resonates with customers. Embrace your uniqueness, focus on what truly sets you apart, and adapt to your customers' evolving needs and expectations to achieve long-term sales success.

## CHAPTER 3: EMOTIONAL SELLING

The Importance of Emotional Selling in Sales:

1. The Logical and Emotional Sale: Both logical and emotional components exist in sales, but emotions hold greater power in compelling action and decision-making.

2. Limitations of Logical Selling: Relying solely on logical selling can lead to missed opportunities, as emotions significantly influence buying decisions.

3. Understanding Emotional Selling: Emotional selling involves filling the prospect's emotional bucket with their own voice and motivations, driven by emotions rather than the salesperson's voice or logical arguments.

4. Dynamics of Emotional Selling: The emotional bucket is infinite, constantly changing, and prone to leaks. A decline in client engagement may indicate an emptying emotional bucket, leading to decreased interest.

5. Importance of Emotional Selling: Emotional selling is crucial as it drives action, sustains the sales process, establishes relationships, builds trust, and increases the likelihood of repeat business and referrals.

6. The Role of Trust in Emotional Selling: Trust is essential in emotional selling as it helps prevent emotional leaks and enhances the depth of the relationship.

7. Refilling the Emotional Bucket: Emotional buckets need continuous refilling, even after an initial positive interaction. Actively listening, encouraging prospects to express their motivations, and finding new ways to engage emotionally are essential for maintaining a filled emotional bucket.

## The E.A.R.N.I.N.G. Sale System

The E.A.R.N.I.N.G. Sale System is a strategic approach to sales that guides salespeople in effectively engaging prospects and leading them to make a buying decision. The system consists of the following steps:

**E: Evaluate** - Gather data and understand the prospect's current reality.

**A: Advantages** - Discover the advantages of the prospect's current solution and build rapport. They are telling you their hot buttons.

**R: Revise** - Identify pain points and areas for improvement to position yourself as a problem solver.

**N: No** - Determine decision-makers and influencers to focus efforts on the right individuals.

**I: Interpret** - Actively listen and repeat the prospect's statements to demonstrate understanding and build trust.

**N: Nothing** - Explore the consequences of maintaining the status quo to create a sense of urgency.

**G: Gain** - Emphasize the gains and benefits the prospect can achieve by adopting your solution to motivate them to move forward with the buying decision.

By following the E.A.R.N.I.N.G. Sale System, sales professionals can effectively engage prospects, address their needs, and build strong relationships, leading to successful sales outcomes. This systematic approach helps salespeople stay customer-centric and persuasive throughout the sales process.

For a free printable version of the E.A.R.N.I.N.G. Sale System, visit www.convertsalesfaster.com.

## CHAPTER 4: SHOW UP, THROW UP

1. Efficient Use of Time:

   - Time is a critical factor in sales interactions, just as it is in a doctor's appointment.

   - Make the most of your limited time with prospects by focusing on their needs and objectives.

2. The Importance of Diagnosis:

   - Before prescribing a solution, a doctor must understand the patient's symptoms, concerns, and history.

   - Similarly, in sales, asking relevant questions and listening attentively to diagnose the prospect's needs and challenges are essential.

3. Avoid the "Show Up, Throw Up" Approach:

   - The "show up, throw up" approach involves monopolizing the conversation with self-focused information and accomplishments.

- Instead, focus on engaging the prospect by asking questions and actively listening to their responses.

4. Talk Less, Listen More:

- Whoever is talking is buying.

- Encourage the prospect to speak and share their thoughts, which indicates their engagement and interest in what you're selling.

5. Let the Prospect Fill Their Emotional Bucket:

- By allowing the prospect to articulate their needs and concerns, they become emotionally invested in finding a solution.

- Personalized and meaningful conversations help build rapport, trust, and motivation for the prospect to take action.

6. Skip the Bragging:

- Avoid excessive self-promotion and focus on the prospect's needs.

- Instead of boasting about achievements or accolades, ask permission to skip over the self-praise and dive into meaningful questions and discussions.

7. Confidence through Humility:

- Demonstrating humility by focusing on the prospect's needs showcases confidence and genuine interest in helping them.

- Let the prospect's voice be heard and create a buying atmosphere by prioritizing their concerns over self-promotion.

8. The Power of Effective Questioning:

    - Effective questioning helps uncover the prospect's pain points, motivations, and desired outcomes.

    - By asking relevant questions, you gain valuable insights to guide the sales process and build a stronger connection with the prospect.

Remember, successful selling requires understanding the prospect's perspective, actively listening, and addressing their specific needs. Focusing on the prospect and creating a collaborative dialogue increases your chances of closing successful deals and fostering long-term customer relationships.

## THE 7-STEP SELLING CYCLE

A framework for successful sales interactions, if you follow the 7-Step Selling Cycle and master each stage, you can effectively navigate the sales process, build strong relationships with prospects, address objections, and ultimately achieve successful outcomes in your sales endeavors.

1. Data Gather:

    - Before approaching prospects, gather relevant information about them, their industry, and their company.

- Look for unique insights or "silver bullets" that can differentiate your approach and provide value to the prospect.

2. First Contact:

   - Once you have information about the prospect, initiate the first contact or approach.

   - This can be done through phone calls, Zoom meetings, or face-to-face interactions.

   - Utilize the silver bullets gathered in the previous step to connect with the prospect.

3. Foundation:

   - Building a strong foundation is crucial for successful sales.

   - Focus on establishing a relationship and trust with the prospect.

   - Use the E.A.R.N.I.N.G. Sales System and dig-in questions to figure out your prospect's what and why.

4. Pitch:

   - The pitch is the stage where you present your proposal or illustration.

   - Blend logical and emotional sales techniques to communicate your product or service's value effectively.

   - Address the prospect's "why" and align your offering with their specific needs.

5. Answer Objections:

- Anticipate objections the prospect may raise and be prepared to address them.

- Overcome objections by providing relevant information, addressing concerns, and offering solutions.

6. Close:

- The close is where you agree on the next step in the sales process.

- It can involve finalizing the sale or moving forward with a specific action plan.

7. Ask for Referrals:

- After successfully closing a sale, leverage the opportunity to ask for referrals.

- Satisfied customers can provide valuable leads and help expand your network.

Flexibility and confidence are required in sales since you'll always encounter different sales scenarios. Understand the loop and have confidence in your approach, knowing that positive results will follow.

## CHAPTER 5: DATA GATHER

Silver Bullets in the Sales Process

1. Understanding Silver Bullets:

- Silver bullets are something you know that the average Joe on the street doesn't know.

- They are crucial in establishing a connection and differentiating yourself from competitors.

2. Extracting Silver Bullets from Referrals:

   - Ask specific questions during the referral-gathering stage to uncover silver bullets.

   - Start with general inquiries and gradually progress to more targeted questions to extract valuable insights.

3. The Value of Silver Bullets:

   - Accumulate as many silver bullets as possible to enhance communication effectiveness.

   - Silver bullets hold significant value in various communication channels, such as phone calls and face-to-face meetings.

4. Utilizing Silver Bullets in Communication:

   - Deploy silver bullets strategically during the first contact or when leaving voicemails to increase callback rates.

   - Craft personalized voicemail messages that include impactful silver bullets to pique curiosity.

5. Leveraging Silver Bullets for Success:

   - Silver bullets transform referrals into valuable connections, so aim to gather at least one or two silver bullets per referral.

6. Handling Referral Callbacks:

- When a referral calls you back, establish control and professionalism instead of immediately launching into a sales pitch.

- Express gratitude for the call, indicate your interest, and schedule a specific time for a focused discussion.

By effectively utilizing silver bullets in the sales process, you can enhance your confidence, engagement, and success in building relationships with prospects and referrals. Adapt the techniques and examples in this appendix to suit your sales approach and industry-specific context.

## CHAPTER 6: FIRST CONTACT

The First Contact with New Prospects

1. The Value of Using a Script:

- Using a script instills confidence, keeps conversations on track, promotes active listening, and ensures consistency in the sales process.

2. Tailoring and Personalizing the Script:

- Use familiar language to create a comfortable atmosphere during the initial contact.

- Engage curiosity by pausing strategically after introducing yourself.

- Acknowledge the prospect's thoughts to establish rapport and empathy.

3. Unveiling Silver Bullets:

   - Leverage referrals and share positive traits or anecdotes about the prospect to add credibility and personalize the conversation.

   - Use silver bullets to emotionally engage clients.

4. Transitioning to Qualification and Next Steps:

   - Address the prospect's mindset by waiting for them to wonder how to end the call, indicating their interest.

   - Introduce a transition statement that conveys your intent to ask qualifying questions and spark curiosity.

   - Begin asking qualifying questions after a brief pause, maintaining a conversational flow.

By incorporating these guidelines into your sales approach, you can make a strong first impression and engage effectively with new prospects. Remember to adapt and personalize the script to align with your style and your prospects' specific needs while consistently delivering your message.

## CHAPTER 7: FOUNDATION

The Importance of Laying Out the Foundation in the 7-Step Selling Cycle

Building a Strong Foundation:

- Eliminate distractions and set the stage for focused interactions.

- Build rapport by using other people's names and making relevant points.

- Uncover the prospect's needs through the E.A.R.N.I.N.G. Sale System.

- Create a buying atmosphere where your prospect has the permission to say no.

- Address objections by anticipating them and having prepared responses.

Ask Dig-In Questions to Fill the Emotional Bucket:

- Engage prospects by letting them talk and express their concerns, desires, and motivations.

- Use dig-in questions to prompt prospects to share more and dig deeper into their needs and motivations.

- Examples of dig-in questions include:

  - Can you tell me more?

  - What does that look like? When you say ____, what do you mean by that?

  - Can you give me an example?

  - Can you say that again?

  - What else?

Tearing Down Walls and Gaining Trust:

- Help prospects tear down their walls by asking dig-in questions and addressing objections.

- Lower prospects' defenses to foster a true partnership and gain their trust.

Filling and Refilling the Emotional Bucket:

- Let prospects fill their emotional buckets by answering questions and expressing their desires.

- Take notes during meetings to remember what prospects want and why they want it.

- Refer to previous conversations to keep prospects engaged and move forward with stalled deals.

Handling Questions Midstride:

- What your prospect ask is important, but why they ask it is extremely important.

- Uncover the prospect's underlying needs and motivations by asking follow-up questions.

- Use dig-in questions to continue the conversation and gather valuable information.

Lead Your Prospects to Solutions:

- Apply the CHIP Method (Cut, Hurt, Intensify, Present) to effectively address prospect issues or challenges.

- Deepen the pain points and present your solution as the answer to their problems.

Create a Comfortable Environment:

- Establish a comfortable environment from the beginning of interactions.

- Seek permission to ask why questions and understand prospects' desires and motivations.

- Set expectations and gain their permission to make the emotional sale.

By understanding and implementing these strategies, sales professionals can lay a strong foundation for successful sales interactions. Remember to adapt these techniques to suit your individual style and the specific needs of your prospects while keeping the focus on building emotional connections and trust throughout the selling cycle.

## CHAPTER 8: PITCH

Your Pitch:

- Your pitch should focus on the prospect's wants and why they want it.

- Tailor your pitch to align with the prospect's stated desires and motivations.

- Keep your pitch short and concise, addressing only the features and benefits relevant to the prospect's specific interests.

- Use your pitch to connect the logical aspects of your product or service to the prospect's emotional needs.

- Close the sale as early as possible, tying your pitch to the prospect's emotional bucket.

Sales Audit:

- Conduct a sales audit to ensure you consistently cover the essential steps within the 7-Step Sales Cycle and fill both the logical and emotional buckets in every sale.

- Use the audit to identify key elements within your pitch that must be addressed.

- Ask yourself questions about the pitch, such as the number of dig-in questions asked, when the prospect moved above the buying line, and if the close was attempted at the right time. For example:
  - How many dig-in questions did I ask?
  - When did they get above the buying line?
  - Did I close them?
  - Did I get them to say what they wanted?
  - Did I get them to say why they wanted it?
  - Did I get them to say what it would be like if that issue was fixed?
  - Did I get them to say what their job would be like if it was fixed?
  - How many trial close questions did I ask?
  - How much time did I spend asking questions for them to fill their logical bucket?
  - How much time did I spend asking questions for them to fill their emotional bucket?
  - Who did most of the talking?
  - Can you write down what they wanted?
  - Can you write down why they want it in their own words?
  - Did you sell to their why?
- Evaluate if you successfully elicited what the prospect wanted, why they wanted it, and how their situation would improve if their needs were met.

- Assess the balance of time spent filling the prospect's logical and emotional buckets.

- Pay attention to the amount of talking you did versus the prospect. Whoever is talking is buying.

By analyzing and documenting your responses to these questions for multiple pitches, you can increase your self-awareness, improve your pitch delivery, and ensure you effectively address both the logical and emotional aspects of the sale.

Note: The specific questions provided are examples, and you can customize them based on your sales process and the unique requirements of your product or service. The sales audit helps you identify areas for improvement and refine your approach to achieve consistent success in sales.

## CHAPTER 9: ANSWER OBJECTIONS

The Three Reasons Why Prospects Don't Buy:

1. Lack of familiarity and likability.

2. Lack of belief in the product or service.

3. Perceived lack of benefit or value.

Address these underlying reasons proactively to increase your chances of making a sale.

The Four Different Types of Objections:

1. Dollars: Financial concerns or perceived high cost.

2. Decider: Wanting external validation or involving someone else in decision-making.

3. Delays: Contentment with the current situation and a reluctance to change.

4. Desire: Uncovering and addressing the prospect's emotional needs and desires.

Identify the objection type to address it effectively and expedite the sales process.

The Formula for Handling Objections—A Seven-Step Approach:

1. Hear them out: Listen attentively to understand the objection fully.

2. Repeat it back: Clarify the objection by repeating it back to the prospect.

3. Box them in: Narrow down the objections and focus on the core challenge.

4. Transition: Acknowledge the objection and smoothly transition to the next step.

5. Make the resell: Understand the prospect's needs and motivations through open-ended questions to refill their emotional buckets.

6. Weak, strongest, stronger: Relate the objection to the prospect's experiences and strengths.

7. Reclose: Close the deal by offering a fresh perspective and presenting the value proposition in a new light.

Adapt the formula to suit your unique sales interactions, and remember that objections present opportunities for growth and success. You can build trust, address concerns, and increase your sales effectiveness by effectively handling objections.

# CHAPTER 10: CLOSE

Strategies for Successful Closing

Preparation for the Close:

- Guide your prospects through the entire selling cycle, ensuring emotional buy-in and clarity on their wants and needs.

- Treat the close as a natural progression in the sales process, not the finish line.

Confidence Required:

- Build confidence by memorizing a word-for-word close to stay focused and present during the closing stage.

- Maintain assertiveness, avoid passivity, and stay fully engaged in the conversation.

Closing Early:

- Consider closing earlier in the sales presentation to increase your chances of success.

- Assume the sale after building rapport and addressing your prospects' needs, but be prepared to address objections if they arise.

Using Trial Closes:

- Incorporate trial closes strategically throughout the sales cycle to gauge your prospect's interest and readiness.

- Trial closes help you determine when your prospects are ready to say "yes" and move forward.

In Conclusion:

- Mastering the art of the close requires preparation, confidence, and strategic use of trial closes.

- Approach the close with a calm and focused mindset, alleviating unnecessary pressure.

- Remember that the close is a natural progression if emotional and logical needs have been addressed.

- Practice closing techniques, ensure full emotional and logical buckets, and embrace the assumptive close.

## CHAPTER 11: ASKING FOR REFERRALS

- Referrals are crucial for exponential growth: While many sales professionals become experts in various aspects of the sales process, they often overlook the importance of asking for referrals. When asking for referrals reaches the same level of expertise as other sales skills, it can lead to significant business growth.

- Shift your mindset: When selling to qualified prospects, you project a positive, confident demeanor. The same mindset should apply when asking for referrals. Avoid being passive or hesitant in your ask. Referrals are more important than the sale itself.

- Referrals have tremendous value: Joe Pallo shares two examples from personal experience where a single referral led to a substantial number of clients. Referrals can open doors and generate extensive business opportunities that otherwise would be difficult to acquire.

- Trust is essential for referrals: Building trust with clients is crucial for successful sales and equally important for receiving referrals. Trust levels required for referrals are often lower than those needed for making a sale.

- Fear of asking for referrals is illogical: Many salespeople fear asking for referrals because they believe it might embarrass clients or damage relationships. However, the fear is often unfounded. Most clients are willing to provide referrals if you approach them professionally and have established trust.

- Anticipate and address objections: Like handling objections during the sales process, it is essential to anticipate and address potential objections when asking for referrals. Objections may include concerns about embarrassment, lack of trust, potential harm to business relationships, or difficulty thinking of suitable referrals.

- Script your referral request: Start with a script and practice it until it becomes natural. The script should include a transition statement, ways to address objections, specific asks for referrals, and a feedback component to keep the conversation ongoing.

- Referrals require a planned approach: Treat asking for referrals like a sale. Just as you follow a process for prospecting, setting appointments, conducting meetings, and closing a sale, referrals should be integrated into your sales plan.

- Collect referrals with a Silver Bullet: When clients provide names of referrals, avoid interrupting or asking additional questions that might disrupt their thought process. Collect the names first and show appreciation. Only delve into more details once they have finished providing all the names.

By implementing these key takeaways and changing your mindset toward asking for referrals, you can leverage the power of referrals to drive significant growth in your business.

## CHAPTER 12: WHAT VERSUS WHY

- What, Why, and How: While knowing what you want and writing it down are essential, understanding why you want it is extremely important. A strong "why" can drive action and overshadow the details of the "what" and "how."

- Vision plays a key role in emotional engagement. Create a vision board or goal notebook using visual aids to stimulate the mind. By focusing on the "be, do, and have" elements, one can shape your vision and involve their family and spouse in the process.

- Include your spouse and kids in creating your vision board to provide motivation and shared goals.

- Prioritize clarifying your vision and understanding your "why." Filling the emotional bucket is essential for meaningful action and transformation.

# B: Acknowledgments

WANT TO THANK the first person who said: "You should write a book." Allison (King) Gruber, it was many years ago, but you got me started.

It follows that I should thank the second and third persons who said: "Joe, I really hate to say this, especially to you, but I think you got something here." Two different people, yet the exact same words. Thank you, Matt Brandt and Taun Olson.

I believe it is customary to thank the editor, that is true, but Henry DeVries is awesome. He is a true "student of the game" and can get more out of people than they think is in them.

Finally, thanks to my wife and kids. Lisa, you have put up with me for years, kept me laughing, raised our kids, and managed to stay sane. You are my best friend; you're neat.

And it's weird that within two weeks, I've had several conversations with some key, very important people who helped me finish the last chapter. Because of their insight, questions, and ability to change my thinking, I could finish the book. And it may be awkward or inappropriate to mention people or give them acknowledgments or dedications at the end of the book, but I'm going to because they really made this happen. Without them, I don't think you would be reading this.

Patrick McGowan was the first person who really got me realigned and engaged after the book sat there for more than a year. Patrick challenged me by saying, "Joe, you have a top-tier and top-shelf service, you are good at what you do, and your clients love you. What part of your business are you okay with being, 'Oh, that's good enough'?"

That's a huge insight there.

Why would you compromise?

Nancy Juetten started talking to me, and I sent her a galley copy of my book within twenty-four hours.

She called me and had many ideas, thoughts, insight, and energy. She is a pro. That lady has two speeds—on and off. When she is engaged, it's at a hundred miles per hour. She's awesome and just fired me up and excited me about finishing it.

Theresa Ashby is phenomenal. She took the time to understand me and the book. She motivated me by understanding what I was trying to do and said, "This is good; you need to get this out."

Chandler Lewis, a founder of 360 Social Impact Studios, was a client of mine, and he said, "Joe, if you're not proud of this book, you can't let it end that way. You can't let it go down on a sour note. If you're not ready, you got to wait, but you also have to do something to make it better." It was a little bit positive and a little bit negative, but it made me realize I won't do anything until I fix the problem.

Jeff Sasse and Brad Koland, two engineers (not sales guys) were sent electronic copies. They both printed them out and edited the whole thing. Both made a similar comment, "This is rare for an engineer to say about a sales book, but this needs to get out."

Christopher Hodges, another author who challenged me. He said, "Joe, why are you writing this?" And he wouldn't give up on it. He started coaching me and he is an awesome coach.

And lastly, but not least, Holli Lawrence. She has touched every part of this book and kept me on track. You would not be reading this without her assistance.

# C: About The Author

JOE PALLO EARNED his BS from North Dakota State University. He financed his education by selling books door-to-door for the Southwestern Company of Nashville, Tennessee. He recruited and developed other college students to run their own individual sales organizations under his leadership.

Joe was a sales trainer with the Tom James Company and has worked with numerous startups and family-run businesses. In addition, he has participated in more than thirty thousand face-to-face selling situations and enjoys working with organizations, helping them develop and enhance a variety of sales programs.

In 2017, Joe began taking his own advice and started his own company, Sell Nothing, LLC. Sell Nothing was created through Joe's passion for helping businesses in the areas of sales coaching, training, and consulting. As a coach, he focuses on understanding and implementing basic sales principles. Then he adds a level of accountability; by combining these two key ideas, he gets more out of his clients than they think is in them. His areas of expertise range from nonprofits to defense contractors, from financial services, insurance to mortgage brokers, and from wholesaling to entrepreneurs and business executives.

Joe is married to his best friend, Lisa. They reside in Shoreview, Minnesota, and have four children. Evidence of his overachiever personality, their goal was to have three.

Joe enjoys reading, camping, cooking, and carpentry in his spare time.

Visit Joe's website at: www.SellNothing.co

Greater Minneapolis–St. Paul, Minnesota Area

# D: ENDNOTES

1. Dale Carnegie, *How to Win Friends and Influence People* (New York: Simon and Schuster, 1946).

Made in the USA
Monee, IL
16 August 2023

41106652R00111